Writing
Step by Step

Other Allison & Busby "Writers' Guides"

Writing
Step by Step

by
Jean Saunders

A practical guide

ALLISON & BUSBY

Published by W.H. Allen & Co. Plc

An Allison & Busby book
Published in 1989 by
W. H. Allen & Co. Plc
Unit 26, Grand Union Center,
338 Ladbroke Grove,
London W10 5AH
Reprinted 1990

Printed and bound in Great Britain by
Cox & Wyman Ltd., Reading, Berkshire

ISBN 0 85031 840 8

Contents

Introduction

Anyone who ever put pen to paper and wrote a series of coherent sentences can logically be called a writer. This is an occupation that conveys the impression of a slightly mysterious being to everyone else, and which many people don't consider as being work at all. Times without number, writers will be asked if they also have "a proper job" . . . . So—what is a writer?

> "Someone who just sits in front of a typewriter all day and waits for the muse to arrive. . . ."
> Someone a little arty who swans around in kaftans and sandals, spouting poetry at every opportunity. . . ."
> "Oh, rich and glamorous, and living in splendid isolation. . . ."

Well, yes, there are a few that fit each of those descriptions. But the term "writer" is a blanket coverage for an extremely diverse body of people, nationwide, who are intensely interested in doing what they love best, which of course, is simply writing. Many of them don't do it for the money, which may be miniscule or spectacular. Many do it for the sheer pleasure of constructing phrases that sing in the senses; that make a reader laugh or bring a tear to the eye; or can make someone sigh with regret when the last page of a novel has been reluctantly turned.

Writers can be poets, newspaper journalists, historical novelists, and Western and science-fiction writers; or simply housewives who send interesting little anecdotes in to magazines and make a surprising amount of pin-money at it. All are writers to some degree. Even the person who works extremely hard at expressing himself on paper, and yet unfortunately never manages to get anything published, is still a writer.

1

The expected outward appearance of this strange being seems to confuse many people—for some reason they expect writers to come rubber-stamped and instantly recognizable. Would you be able to pick out a bank manager in a crowd? Or a telephone engineer or a computer expert or a sales rep or a typist or. . . .? I was once told scathingly by a rather objectionable prospective house-buyer who was prodding about in my office, "But you don't look like a writer. Not like —————. *She* wears capes and things." "Not around the house, surely," I replied. (Thankfully, for the neighbours' sake, he didn't buy our house.)

A writer is never just a writer. That's what makes it one of the most fascinating professions to be in and, in many ways, one of the most precarious. You don't get a regular income when you're freelance. What you do get is enormous satisfaction in receiving an acceptance letter from an editor; the thrill of a lifetime when you first see your words in print, however humble the piece you sent in, or the publication in which it's printed; the secret or not-so-secret ego trip of walking into any crowded room and knowing that you're probably the only one there who's actually realized a dream.

For many people, writing is a dream that will never be fulfilled. Ask any writer you happen to meet how many times they have been told that an acquaintance always dreamed of writing a book. That someday they too, are going to find the time. They will rattle off some impossible storyline or family history and expect you to be intensely interested. If you've got any sense, you *will* be, because some nugget of information may just spark you off for your next great saga. (But not because you want to take on the task of writing up their life story for them, which some expect . . . turn the tables at once, and tell them it would be far more fascinating told as an autobiography.)

A writer is interested in people. How else can their own stories come alive with human interest? This applies to every kind of writing, not just fiction. Newspaper stories with screaming headlines that tear at the heart-strings may be written by an apparently tough reporter, but that person must have a genuine interest in people to put just the right amount of compassion into their writing. Of course it sells newspapers, but that reporter is also canny enough to know human nature. You hate

2

those over-slushy stories? If the demand wasn't there, news-papers wouldn't print them.

Romantic novelists have been known to weep over their manuscripts—oh yes, I've done it—and far from sneering at this trait, I believe it proves that the writer is writing from the heart and not just the head—or with the merry sound of cash-tills in the background.

You may then ask why a factual textbook needs to be written with human interest: surely all that is required are the facts, written up in a clear, concise way? True, but who is going to read these dry and dusty facts if not people? And unless they're written in a reasonably entertaining manner, the student will soon tire of the bald words.

The most successful articles are those slanted for the parti-cular needs of the readers of magazines. You wouldn't expect to find a piece about fly-fishing in a teenage pop magazine, would you? That's an extreme example, but so often a little more thought as to where to send your work, or to rewrite it in a way that appeals to the publication's readership, will make all the difference between acceptance and rejection.

Writing is as old as time. Those early scribes who scratched away on stone and slate may not have had the circulation figures of modern newspaper giants or popular publishing houses, but their work was as eagerly awaited in meeting-place and market square as any early morning edition.

The Bible is the most widely read book in the world, printed in many languages, types and presentations. But the very first printed book that history records is the *Diamond Sutra*, a Bud-dhist scripture consisting of a sixteen-foot scroll and printed in May, 868. It is a priceless find that didn't come to light until the year 1900, being walled up in one of the Caves of the Thousand Buddhas in Turkestan with many other manuscripts of a bygone and forgotten age. It's a humbling thought that although time passes, and bones decay, the written word remains.

Writing means many things to many people: a way of earning their living; an enjoyable part-time occupation that brings in the occasional small cheque; and the glamour of being famous and successful, which do not necessarily go together. It can defi-nitely be a kind of therapy—many people with personal prob-

3

lems have turned to writing to "get it all out of their system", whether for publication or not.

Rather more obscure to non-writers, is the cameraderie that exists between writers. There is the sharing of success and failure, the social contact from the many organizations and conventions that exist to bring like-minded people together for a brief while before they return to the sheer hard slog of finishing that chapter, or juggling with those elusive words to bring that epic poem to life.

Oh, you thought it was all easy? That this is going to be a book that paints a picture of someone happily tapping away on a typewriter with two fingers of one hand (while stirring the gravy with the other), and publishers telephoning daily with offers that only an idiot could refuse?

Gentle reader, you have a lot to learn.

But the aim of this book is not to put you off. Instead, it is an attempt to show you, step by step, how a writer can progress from the simplest submissions to magazine or newspaper to the enormity and grandeur of writing historical sagas, or to any point in between. For one of the delights of our profession is the freedom of choice to write whatever you wish and still be called a writer.

You will not find these chapters geared especially to any one aspect of writing, nor solely to writing itself. There are omissions of which I have no writing knowledge, such as science fiction. There are also many peripheral activities in which a writer becomes involved, such as successful self-promoting, which are included as light relief from all the hard work and perseverance that goes into a writer's craft.

So now, read on. . . .

Jean Saunders

1

Small is Sweet

You may think that small pieces do not deserve to be called "Real Writing" and are not worth submitting, but I assure you that they bring enormous pleasure to many people who have little time for writing. The rewards are the modest amounts of money or, in some cases, prizes, given by magazines and newspapers.

If you've never attempted to write anything before, and have no grandiose ambition to be a novelist and no inclinations to do the hard graft of writing factual articles, what else is there for a beginner to try? I am now assuming that you would like to get into print, and to have your name beneath something in a magazine. Also that you don't have too much time to devote to what may be a new and interesting idea of being a writer.

The Letters Page

The starting point for many people is the letters page of magazines and newspapers. Not "Real Writing", you cry once more (perhaps speaking from experience of the one or two letters you've already sent off, never to hear of them again). Perhaps you've simply discarded any more notions of sending letters to the press, suspecting that they're all staff-written anyway, under a series of *noms de plume*. This is not so. Because such publications are inundated with entries such as yours, they can pick and choose the best of them, so don't dismiss letter-writing as being not worth your time and effort, when others are doing quite nicely from them, thank you.

You may think you're doing no more than sitting down and writing a breezy letter, outlining something amusing that happened to you, and even if you have a sneaky feeling that it doesn't read back to you in *quite* such an entertaining way, and it's a bit long-winded and wordy, you send it off anyway. After all, Great Aunt Ethel laughed at it when you told her about it. . . . However, someone else writing up that same incident may do it in a far more acceptable way than you, in publishing terms. That other writer may know just how to keep the story brief, perhaps within the publication's usual 50–100 words; how to make the maximum impact on a busy editor by choosing visual words that say everything in a phrase instead of waffling on with several sentences; how to start and how to finish, encapsulating that hilarious moment for a reader who wasn't there at the time but, because of the succinct way the letter is worded, will feel as though he was. This is the letter that will be published.

A letter I once had published in a magazine concerned a village cricket scene. It was a simple, true incident, easy for a reader to follow and conjuring up a picture. It went as follows:

> My brother-in-law was playing cricket for the local village team. He rubbed the ball against his trouser leg to clean away the grass, forgetting that he had some book matches in the pocket. The friction ignited the matches, and when he'd put out the fire he was left with a singe on his cricket whites, and a perfectly square hairless patch on his leg. Some match!

This letter was one of my first efforts in writing and earned me a small sum of money. It was published in a women's magazine about twenty years ago, but would probably still sell today, because the cricket scene is timeless. Below is an objective analysis of the letter.

It's short and to the point. The first sentence states exactly what the letter is about. The next gives the reader a sense of anticipation that something is about to happen. The third sentence gives the answer to the question in the reader's mind and is lengthy enough for him to savour it. The final sentence is as brief as possible, to punch home the point and to provide contrast with the previous one. The entire tone of this letter is snappy.

The sentences intentionally vary in length, and the pun at the end lifts the reader and either brings a smile or a groan. The letter was sent to a magazine that used both male and female anecdotes, and which particularly liked the human-interest aspect on their letters page.

Another published letter went like this:

> A recent article in your newspaper discussed the merits of packet-tea or tea-bags. Some of your readers would prefer space to be used for more intelligent matter, and not such drivel. Compared with the excellent piece on nuclear disarmament, wouldn't you say it all seemed like a bit of a storm in a tea-cup?

This one was obviously more belligerent, and sent to a newspaper that welcomed a controversial post-bag and wasn't afraid of publishing letters against itself.

Analysis: again, the first sentence pin-points the content of the letter. The letter-writer speaks for other readers, thus inviting a possible on-going correspondence, which this particular newspaper enjoys. The last sentence ends with a bit of dry wit that neatly ties up the whole letter.

There's no need to go on at length when you can say everything you want to say in a short piece, and you're more likely to get it published because the editor will have more space to use more letters and give his readers a variety of writers' comments. Naturally, if you intended sending letters to a publication that regularly used longer epistles, you would tailor yours to that market.

The next letter gives a different slant:

> Some rather grand Canadian friends were visiting us recently. Tongue-in-cheek, the husband announced that he had decided to give us an award. Our hearts swelled. Was it for top-class cuisine? Genteel hospitality? Comfort at all times? No. Ours was the first bathroom he'd been in where the toilet-roll holder was in the right place.

Analysis: first sentence states the topic; the next one anticipates. Then a touch of pride on the part of the letter-writer, and the options given to the reader are gracious and dignified. Finally comes the crunch, with a longer sentence describing the actual remark. The important element of this letter is one that will gladden the heart of many an editor. The writer is laughing at herself. Poking gentle fun at yourself is always more acceptable than poking fun at other people. Laugh with them, as in the first letter, but not at them.

The above three letters alone may give you some idea of the vast range of styles and incidents that can be covered by such submissions. Of course, many people happily write their letters without ever considering that this could be a small cottage industry in itself. The plain fact is that if you want to make a mini-career out of publishing your letters, it pays to study the techniques of making them saleable.

To sum up. Always aim for the correct magazine or newspaper—"market studies" is a phrase that every aspiring writer comes across sooner or later, and it applies just as much to the simple art of letter-writing for publication, as to not sending your magnificent family saga to a publisher that only specializes in children's books.

An excellent reference book is the *Writers' & Artists' Yearbook*, published annually by A. & C. Black. Contrary to what the beginner may think, this is not only a tome for the experienced writer. It's also an essential book for the beginner as it not only lists magazines and newspapers but gives their addresses, the lengths and styles of features used, and in many cases, payment. Entries give an insight to the general content of the publications, and some also mention their readership and whether or not photographs are required to go with articles. Since the book is published annually, and magazines in particular come and go like the tide, it pays to buy a revised copy from time to time, or look up the current one at your library. Most writers consider it an invaluable addition to their bookshelf, since it also contains the names and addresses of agents and publishers (both British and foreign) as well as articles on copyright, tax, and so on.

From time to time, I will be recommending various books that will be of use for the reader who intends to pursue writing more seriously. But letter-writing can be considered one of the simpler ways of breaking into print—and although the writers are people sitting at home like you and me, never let it be thought that the content of all those letters you read are exactly as it happened. You don't have to have discovered some secret gem of information that will dazzle readers, or write up some amusing anecdote of your darling child. Write up a short piece that is entertaining, and you are in effect writing a story in miniature. Which is basically just what a letter is.

When it comes to market studies, you can't beat buying magazines and newspapers and seeing the kind of letters and small features they prefer. Since you can't buy every one, concentrate on sending your letters to the publications you like to read, because you'll already be on their wavelength and will have gleaned something of the editor's preferences from published items.

Before we go any further, a bit about how you actually send in your work. You may not have realized until now that there are people making a serious career of writing letters for publication. You may never know how many of those names you see beneath the letters are genuine. Letter-writers are just as likely to use a variety of names as novelists are to use different pen-names.

No magazine wants to use the same letter-writer week after week, but Joe Bloggs can become Mrs Ariadne de Grenville, or Lady Flannery or Sue Pink—and in reality they can all be Mrs Binnie Bunn, housewife, sending out a selection of letters and getting them all printed, and receiving four cheques for her ingenuity.

Never send out the same letter to different publications. Yes, it has been done, but editors don't take kindly to duplication, and most request and expect that all letters should be original. If an editor discovers you've been duplicating, they may well throw out anything else you submit.

So, having realized that letter-writing is being done by thousands of other hopefuls, what else can you do to make the editor stop and read yours? Presentation is the word. If you possibly can, always type your letters. It doesn't really matter whether you use single- or double-spacing in this case, as long as the letter is neatly presented, clear to read, and is a joy for any editor to open on a wet Monday morning.

Obviously, not everyone can type or has access to a typewriter, so make your letter as legible as you can. Don't scribble it in pencil, or indelible ink that makes the editor's fingers purple for the rest of the day. Don't include an additional letter about yourself and your cat, or information about which no one but your family wil have the remotest interest. Your letter intended for publication may be just a simple anecdote, but professional eyes will be assessing it before it ever gets into print, and all that the editor is interested in is the effect it will have on their readers. There's no point in sending a stamped, addressed envelope for your letter's return, since those that are unused end up in the waste-paper basket.

So how long can you reasonably wait before sending it out to another potential market? Magazines are printed well in advance of publication, and it may be weeks or months before your letter is chosen, depending on whether the magazine is a weekly or monthly. I would never bother to try the same letter again. Write another one, on a similar topic if you like, but make it different from the first. Try to keep up a flow of letters to different markets, and keep a copy of each and a record of where you've sent them. Start off by being businesslike, good practice for when you turn to other types of writing where you will undoubtedly be competing with the professionals. Keeping proper records and copies of your letters will also keep your mind fresh for new ideas, get you in the mood for writing, and let you see how your own technique is improving.

Although you shouldn't send the same letter to different publications, the same *idea* can be used many times. For instance, look again at the cricket anecdote above. I could have written it up quite seriously for a health or sports publication, pointing out the dangers of matches in trouser pockets. Or hilariously, imagining setting fire to a more vital part of the anatomy. I could have sent it to a house magazine—perhaps one published for match manufacturers or cricketing gear—or the local newspaper, each time angled to its particular readership. Wittier, it may have sold to a feminist magazine, or in a more sophisticated form to a glossy.

Letter-writing is one way in which small items can get into print. The all-important thing to remember is to write about something that will entertain someone else, which is really what writing is all about.

Puzzles and Crosswords

Letters aren't the only things that take little time and effort. I began my writing career with short stories, which deserve a chapter to themselves, but while I was getting the inevitable rejection slips that come to us all, I was also doing other things. Obviously all writers must have an intense interest in words and I was always intrigued by the idea of writing and constructing word puzzles. I do not profess to be a contender for Mastermind, and such efforts were confined to childrens magazines, mainly a small magazine for Brownies. For these I made up crossword puzzles, and Riddle-Me-Rees, and various simple puzzles that young children could easily understand and solve. Nothing irritates children more than trying to unravel a word puzzle that is far too obscure for them.

Making up crossword puzzles for a young magazine meant using short words, and making the puzzle in a symmetrical pattern. Draw the puzzle first, with a good clear black pencil, making a large square, then dividing it into smaller squares, until you have a basic outline. By filling in some of the small squares, you will end up with a blank crossword outline with connecting words of any length you choose. This simple technique can be used to construct any kind of crossword, from the very small to one of giant proportions as used in *Annabel* magazine.

The secret of compiling a crossword is to fill in the blanks with words first, and to make up the clues afterwards. Thus the words and clues can be made fitting to the readership and the magazine or newspaper for which it is intended. Why not try your own weekly newspaper with a theme suited to your locality?

A word puzzle that is a younger children's favourite is the Riddle-Me-Ree. For *The Brownie* magazine, I used such themes as the following illustration.

My first is in kingdom but not in state,
My second's in evening, not in late,
My third is in stumble but not in fall,
My fourth is in tiny and also in tall,
My fifth is in pencil but not in ink,

11

My sixth is in orange and also in pink,
My whole is an animal, furry and sweet,
Who purrs with contentment and curls at your feet.
Answer . . . KITTEN

I'm sure you can think up many more ideas for yourself. Word Squares are also easy to construct and fill many a corner in a children's magazine or local newspaper. Simply draw a large grid square containing 16 small squares. Find four words that read the same down and across, and give simple clues for the reader to solve.

Poems

Poems are used by many magazines. I don't mean the terribly literary pieces, but the various smaller kinds from the short and zany to the more romantic kind to be found in teenage and women's magazines. The more sophisticated the magazine, the more thoughtful the poems printed. Humorous poems in particular attract the editor's eye and are likely to appeal to readers. So are seasonal ones with a new slant to them—moon and June are drastically overdone—and a poem written from an animal viewpoint, or a child's, or even an inanimate object such as a broom, could be innovative and original. (A broom as a narrator? Why not? Think what it may encounter during a working day. . . .)

All the above suggestions are the very simplest ways of using small items of writing to get your work into print and to make modest amounts of money. You'll never make a fortune out of them, but they can give you a great deal of pleasure and satisfaction. When one of my daughters was only 14 years old, she decided to try writing similar small items, and was as successful in selling them as I was.

Since, even with the smallest amount of work that you send away, you're entering the world of the professional or staff writer, one consideration that must never be overlooked is the need for attention to detail. Spelling, punctuation, grammar, and all those boring things you thought you'd left behind with your schooldays. If you skipped it then, don't skip the next chapter, because you could just be in need of a quick refresher course.

Back to the drawing-board

Yes, it's dreary to think that before you even begin writing, you have to get to know certain procedures. You may be raring to go, your tale burning to be told, and to blazes with any rules and regulations regarding submissions. You may argue that there are tales of writers sending in dog-eared manuscripts that were so wonderful that a publisher snapped them up immediately, and didn't care that they were written on lavatory paper. Don't you believe it! That's the kind of tale that makes colourful reading, but is as unlikely as Shakespeare writing *Twelfth Night* on a word processor. Once upon a time there may have been writers who submitted badly handwritten manuscripts and got them published. But not any more. Those days are gone, along with crinolines and gaslights, and however much we may sigh nostalgically (or not) at the thought of Emily Brontë writing *Wuthering Heights* romantically by candlelight, the facts of a writer's life have changed.

Preparing your work for submission

Submissions of books, fiction and non-fiction, short stories and articles, all have a similar format to follow. They are typed in double-spacing on A4 good-quality paper, using one side of the paper only, and leaving good margins at top, bottom and each side. Each page is numbered consecutively, without getting the pages mixed up when you send them to the publisher of your choice. Always send return postage and a brief covering letter for politeness' sake, which need only say what it is that you're offering, and hoping that it will be suitable for that publisher's requirements. Don't waffle in your letter, or the publisher will automatically be thinking that your story or whatever will waffle too.

Publishers expect to see a script written with intelligence and care, and the writer who can't be bothered to check spelling mistakes and correct them neatly gets a mental black mark. Spelling does not come easily to everyone, but if you're not sure of a word, look it up. (Get the *Bad Spellers' Dictionary* if you're absolutely awful.)

Words are the tools of a writer's trade, but the use of words does not come readily to everyone. *Roget's Thesaurus* (Penguin), is a mine of useful alternatives when searching for an exact meaning in a word without repeating yourself. In describing a character's line of dialogue, for instance, the adjectives "sweetly", "tenderly" and "gently", don't convey exactly the same emotion to the reader. Know the way you want your character to speak in that instance, and use the best word you can to describe it. But don't get so carried away by the thought of a *Thesaurus* that you forget that often a simple word is best.

When you're writing fiction, always begin each new bit of dialogue on a new line, even if it's only two words being said. This separates each person's part in the story, and makes it easier to read and understand. Read your dialogue aloud to ensure that it's natural and applicable to the status, class, personality, age, etc., of the character.

No two people speak alike, or have the same mannerisms. Make your characters instantly recognizable and as individual as real people. Authors should always think of their characters as real people. Listen to the way actors describe the characters they play on stage or film; that's the way you should be thinking of the characters you create in fiction.

For some reason, paragraphing causes one of the biggest headaches to new writers. The two main faults are the obvious. Miss Pedantic will write long, long paragraphs that take up pages and daze the reader with a mass of dense black-and-white prose. Miss Frothy will fill the pages with almost every sentence being a new paragraph on its own, so that the result is a bitty affair that makes the reader suspect there's no real substance in the story anyway.

In many cases, the kind of writing you are doing will dictate the length of paragraphs. Newspaper items will often have only two or three short sentences to a paragraph, sometimes only one. A bright and breezy article may also have short paragraphs, and each one will be leading the reader smoothly on to the next. In very general terms, the more serious the article, the longer the paragraphs will be.

Similarly with fiction. The paragraphs in a children's book will be shorter than those in a romance; and a historical novel will often have the longest paragraphs of all, especially where factual background is interwoven with fictional events. The best way to grasp the use of paragraphing is to study published books, not as a reader, but as a student of how other writers have used paragraphs to their best advantage.

An effective one-liner paragraph often comes at the end of a non-fiction book's chapter, to underline a point.

The one-liner can also draw the reader's attention to some significant comment in a novel.

Perhaps the paragraph's most useful asset is in starting the reader on a new line of thought. Often, when you're writing at full stretch, you get the words down so quickly that you forget to break the sentences up into a pattern at all and it's only later that you realize you've got this great mass of words in front of you. If that is the way you like to work, then at that stage, it doesn't matter. Rather than worrying over where the breaks should go, it's far better to get those words down on paper, and break them up later into a more pleasing pattern at the appropriate sentences. With practice, your own instincts will tell you where they should be.

Right now, I would like to point out that the methods by which writers work are many and diverse. Your own personality and the amount of time you can devote to your writing will eventually decide the method that is right for you. The guides I give in this book have been tried and tested, but all can be ignored if you have already found your own best way. However, back to the drawing-board.

Punctuation

Mistakes in punctuation should be taken seriously. You can make the most horrible gaffes if you are uncertain of the use of punctuation marks, and the last thing you want an editor to do is burst out laughing at one of your dramatic sentences because you've put an essential comma in the wrong place. The following sentence illustrates this.

"With car wheels screeching, Mary gasped and held on tightly as the vehicle went out of control."

"With car wheels, screeching Mary gasped and held on tightly as the vehicle went out of control."

Use of correct punctuation indicates to your readers where you want them to pause. Readers must be allowed to draw breath, to take in important phrases, to know the significance of certain key sentences.

A well-known writer kept up an interesting correspondence in *The Bookseller* a while ago, concerning what he called so effectively "The floating apostrophe". That's the little devil that causes more problems in writing than any other aspect of punctuation.

Should it be it's or its?

I am not intending to try to teach anyone the basics of good grammar, and a more detailed explanation can be found in any good manual of English usage (for example *Hart's Rules for Compositors and Printers*, OUP, 1983, and Judith Butcher's *Copy-editing*, CUP, 1981). But the following sentences are examples of the floating apostrophe correctly used.

It's been a fine day.
It's good weather for October.
(Abbreviations for it has, it is.)

Its origins were unknown.
Jet-lag was still having its effect on her.
(Its—qualifies "origins" and "effect" respectively.)

17

Writing a sentence would seem the simplest of exercises. You merely state what you have to say and insert a full stop at the end. But you've probably read sentences in a novel that seem to go on for ever. By the time you get to the end of them, you've forgotten what the beginning was all about. You're so bewildered you have to keep going back to check up.

Sentences that vary in length retain the reader's interest, but they should also be in keeping with the *kind* of writing involved. Lengthy sentences are more suited to serious novels, though for some reason the writers of computer textbooks seem to think long sentences make things easier to understand. Those who try to understand them certainly don't!

Where you are conveying an impression of fear or sudden crisis in a novel, then the shorter the sentence, the sharper that feeling comes across to the reader. (Don't prolong the sequence unnecessarily, or it will probably give the reader a heart attack.) It's a very good technique to use in thriller-writing where danger threatens, and perhaps the main character suddenly realizes they are no longer alone. For example:

> Slowly, the door-handle began to turn. Mary's hands felt clammy. The breath was tight in her throat. She couldn't breathe. She was sure she was going to faint. She could hear the rasp of someone else's breathing, harsh and thick. It terrified her.

The sixth sentence gives the reader a small moment of relaxation from the tension before the panicky mood of the character takes over again. Compare the above example with another that is written less competently.

> Slowly, the door-handle began to turn and Mary's hands felt clammy. The breath was tight in her throat and also she couldn't breathe and she was sure she was going to faint. She could hear the rasp of someone else's breathing, harsh and thick, and it terrified her.

There is very little difference in those two passages. Only a few extra words are added, yet the lengthy sentences slow down the action and the feeling of rising terror for the character. The first example is taut, the tension taking an upward swing. The second is flat and less interesting, and the reader wouldn't be carried along with the momentum of the scene.

Weaknesses in beginners' writing often come from the use of too many adjectives or adverbs, though I do think that it's a mistake to get rid of some of the lovely words we all favour. The trouble is, we favour them too frequently. We become addicted to our own pet phrases and words. Before we know it, we've used them too often, the reader comes to expect them and becomes bored with them. And a bored reader won't buy your next book.

Word Processors

The advent of word processors has made the weeding out of pet phrases much easier. It's merely a case of asking the magic machine to tell you how many times you've used a certain word and, if it's too many, it will then point out each offending place in the script and you can substitute an alternative. Magic indeed, and a godsend to someone like me, with a penchant for certain words. But this book is not going to be about the mechanics of word processors. There are other books on the market that will tell you how to use them, and give you advice on buying them.

All I will say is that if you ask another writer what benefit a word processor has been to him or her, you will probably be tempted. If you can afford one, get one.

Other writers will inevitably say it has speeded up production, made revision immensely easy instead of being such a chore, and thus improved their writing. I can only concur.

You may be interested in doing what I did. I went to a reputable computer dealer and hired my word processor on a month's trial, with several hours' tuition thrown in. I liked the one I hired so much that I eventually bought it without trying anything else, although I had the use of three printers before I found the one that suited me.

Now, for those of you feeling utterly inadequate because you're still writing in the good old-fashioned way with a pen, or bashing away on a typewriter . . . it doesn't matter an atom. It's the end result that counts . . . and many a successful writer refuses to look at new-fangled machines. You are not alone, and I avoid talking about my word processor as much as possible, with the dread of becoming a word-processor bore . . . so, no more.

Getting started

The old hand won't fail to notice how new writers will offer a score of excuses for why they haven't yet begun. None of the excuses hold water.

You're never too old. Many writers have begun quite late in life. All that matters in the writing world is to produce something that's entertaining to somebody else. That's all. Many older people have a fund of interesting stories to tell: they may have spent years writing interesting letters to family or friends; sometimes they decide to write a book on their reminiscences; sometimes it will strike lucky, and be published.

Never, ever, underestimate the importance of luck in having anything published. A favourite story among writers is how someone was gushing to a famous scribe about how lucky he was to be so successful. "And the harder he worked, the luckier he got . . ." was the now much-quoted reply.

But to be serious about this question of luck. You could send a brilliant article or short story to a magazine, only to have it turned down. Not because the piece wasn't worthy of publication, but because the editor had recently used something with a similar theme. The editor may have something almost identical lined up for the following month. It's no use being incensed when the next issue comes out and making accusations about your idea being stolen because, as I've already said, some magazines go to press months before they appear in the shops.

It's strange how writers can have similar ideas at the same time. Sometimes it's a TV programme that sparks off a thought in a writer's mind, and this thought catches the imagination of others as well. It may be written up in different ways, but suddenly editors will be inundated with pieces about, for instance, surrogate motherhood or space-age romance. It is not the editor's fault that only one such story can be used, and that chosen will be the one that best suits the readership. It's just hard luck on the rest of the writers.

How and where do you work? Moan to a published writer that you never have enough time, or a special quiet corner of the house in which to work, and you'll probably be greeted with a polite smile that hides gritted teeth. We've heard it all before, you see. I began writing on the kitchen table, with a husband, three children, a part-time job, and sundry cats and dogs around the place. Spare time? What was that?

No, dear aspiring writer. If you want to write badly enough, you will write. So away with the excuses and get down to it. Start small, as I did. When the kids grow up, as they eventually will (believe it), graduate to longer works.

Blockbuster novels? How could I ever find time to write those? Now I can, and all those years of apprenticeship with short stories, articles and anything else I could think of to get into print, weren't wasted. They gave me the special confidence you too will discover when an editor writes or phones to tell you they want to publish your work. That's a magical moment indeed.

How long can you write at a stretch? Snatched half hours can certainly limit your concentration, but even professional writers sometimes work no more than a few hours a day. Being a writer is far more tiring than you might think. It's hard on muscles and circulation, it's bad for lack of exercise, your eyes can get glazed and your head can ache. If you're poring over a highly dramatic or emotional scene, your mouth can become very dry because you're breathing through your mouth due to all that concentration . . . at least, it has that effect on me.

Deep breathing is often necessary, and being periodically topped up with cups of coffee or tea (or whatever else you're addicted to) is essential if unwise. Taking a stroll around the house or garden to rest your eyes and legs, which get remarkably stiff from sitting, is also beneficial. Taking time off to talk to

21

your neighbours, dog, husband, wife or children (not necessarily in that order), is helpful too. I'm not joking. I do all of those things. Oh yes, I even talk to my husband. I'm a compulsive writer, but not a recluse.

I do not write in time to the record-player, radio or TV. Some people do. Music as a background is fine, but I'm afraid I'd be singing along with it. Music is a way of relaxation to me, and writing is my work. As recreation I will bash away on the piano, but it's more for my own pleasure than anyone else's. However, if music suits your mood, then write to it.

What I'm pointing out is that you don't *need* any of these props that others may advise. You don't need to live in the country or have the noise of a city outside your office window for the muse to descend on you. The *muse* is a much over-rated commodity bestowed on writers by non-writers. All you need is a pen and paper, an idea, the incentive to knock it into shape, and you're away.

Whatever you do, try to get something finished. There is nothing so satisfying as writing those two magic words "The End". So many writers never reach that stage—they get discouraged, and half-finished manuscripts are pushed out of sight. Nothing ever got published while it was languishing in a cupboard.

Samuel Taylor Coleridge was known to comment that the titles of the books he planned to write would fill a volume. Planning isn't writing, though there's a lot of fun to be had in planning what you intend to write. The acid test is whether or not you ever get it written.

3

Writing Articles

I am now going to assume that you have had a certain amount of success in writing smaller items for publication, and are moderately pleased with the result, including your small personal cuttings file. (You are keeping them, aren't you? On a bad day, they can boost your confidence faster than anything else.)

Are you now ready to tackle something slightly more ambitious? And here I will stress again that in no way do I mean to imply that writing smaller items is of less importance than writing novels or a new *War and Peace*.

Many people plunge right in and write a novel, because that's all they want to do. A very few get their first efforts published and make a fortune. For the vast majority of people who are still struggling to write even *something* saleable, take heart. It's easy to get depressed and think you'll never make it, but you can always try a different direction in writing, remember? While fiction-writing may not be your thing, factual articles just might.

Many of the points already given in Chapter Two on the art of letter-writing for publication apply to article-writing: the importance of the first sentence, the holding of the reader's interest, the denouement and the finale. If some of the points are repeated, it is only because inevitably many aspects of writing in general overlap and are interwoven. Remember, letter-writing was dealt with in detail as a step towards article-writing.

Articles appear in every publication you can name. They provide a constant source of reading pleasure, and many a writer's bread-and-butter. Articles can be written about virtually any subject, which makes them a good way for the beginner to ease into the professional writing market.

"Write about what you know" is an old adage that is meant to apply to all kinds of writing. I heavily dispute it. If it were strictly adhered to, there would be no science fiction and no historical sagas. (Well, what contemporary writer has first-hand knowledge of Elizabethan times, for goodness' sake?) The phrase really doesn't have much meaning for the fiction writer, where the author's own imagination is one of the most valuable assets. Research into facts and background is essential for the historical novelist, and for most other forms of novel-writing as well. I prefer to say that if you don't know your subject, then find out about it before you begin to write. Readers will always spot mistakes, be sure of it.

How does all this apply to the article-writer? Not in quite the same way, though the things that you know best are probably the ideal ones about which to start writing.

Everyone has topics about which he or she is perhaps not an expert, but has some special knowledge. Writing up that information in an amusing or serious manner (depending on the publication for which its slanted) is the way in which many a successful article-writer has got started. For instance, do you enjoy gardening? There are dozens of magazines that welcome amusing gardening anecdotes. Is your new home bordering on farmland so that the scent of pig manure wafts across with the roses? Somebody might just enjoy hearing all about that! Alternatively, housewives or teenagers on a tight budget would love to know how to make some pin money. Unemployed people might be dying to know how *you* coped with similar problems to theirs. A friend of mine published an amusing article on the disappearance of those old curved nappy pins, after struggling with the newer kinds on his baby grandson. (You didn't know they had changed? You do now.)

In all of the above cases, try to have a good number of facts to include in your article. Your own experiences will only be the starting-point, but they will be things that interest you, so be prepared to do a little more research to add a variety of comparisons about, say, the nappy-pin question. Perhaps what other countries use? No? That doesn't inspire you? Then perhaps you could write to the local job centre for any pamphlets on making money at home to include in an article for the unemployed idea.

Inevitably, you will soon have outgrown writing about domestic matters (unless you intend to make that your particular bent), and want to expand your writing skills. Then you will undoubtedly need to research as much for article-writing as for any other field of writing, and you will discover that the most unlikely topics can make interesting articles.

You will also be expanding your own knowledge. One of the by-products of being a writer is the amassing of information in that marvellous computer we call a brain. Another is the ability to keep that brain active, to be always curious and investigative, and never to lose sight of the things that are going on all around us. A writer sees things that other people miss. A writer is someone who is still filled with wonder.

Far-fetched? Romanticized? I know one author who writes highly successful articles about postmarks. Not a topic that would be terribly inspiring, you might think. But written in a lively way by someone with an obvious enthusiasm for postmarks, for the detail that goes into them, the various countries that use them, their differences and similarities and history and entertainment value, his articles bring a seemingly dry subject to life.

Finding ideas for articles would probably present the non-writer with a complete block. For the practised writer, ideas are everywhere. A fiction-writer can find inspiration in the sheen of rain on dark streets; an article-writer on the differences in front doors through the ages; on lamp-posts, old and new; the origin of street names; local customs; bridle-paths; Christian names.

Think of any subject you like, and an article can be written about it. You may know nothing about, for instance, the origin of street names, but you could find out by going to your library and looking up various reference books. More interestingly, you could find old newspapers in your own town, and make the article of local interest with street names that readers would recognize.

Articles can be personal: "Pianos I Have Loved" was a humorous one that I once wrote; "Wigs and Hairpieces" for a girls' magazine was another, as was "The Fascination of Morris Dancing".

25

Articles for specialist magazines are not always written by experts. Anyone with something relevant to say about their product or way of life may be able to construct a saleable article. The "County" magazines, for instance, would be interested in a country feature pertinent to their area.

Many women's magazines are open to freelances for submitting articles and features. The human or humorous angles are those more likely to be accepted, though a well-researched topical theme may sell as well. Always remember the publishing schedule though, and don't submit a Christmas article in November, because the Christmas issue was probably completed in August.

Teenage magazines take a certain number of articles, but in all cases, read the magazine of your choice and see the kind of writing they prefer. It's pointless sending in a piece that's ponderous and heavy, when the magazine concerned only publishes lighthearted work. Teenage magazines may be rather more tricky for an older person because of their subject matter.

There are article-markets in plenty, but how do you write something that will please an editor? With so many people trying to break into print, it's clear that editors can be choosy, and if you want to be sure that it's *your* piece that's chosen, then it's important to interest that editor with your very first words.

The title is the first thing that any reader sees and your first reader is going to be an editor. So make your title relevant, not only to the topic itself but to the publication for which it's intended, and the readership. The magazine you fancy may not be one that you normally read, and you may be doubtful that you could write an article for it, so how do you know who reads such a magazine?

A significant clue lies in the advertisements. If the magazine specializes in advertising upmarket perfumes, Harrods clothes and accessories, and Gucci handbags, you can bet it has a readership that's fairly affluent. If it's a magazine that has nearly every ad devoted to babywear or clothes for the expectant mother, you don't need me telling you that this is a magazine that would be more interested in domestic and family articles than in brass rubbings.

As well as studying the content, advertising, style and readership of a magazine, there's one other very important aspect that the article-writer should not overlook: the length of the articles published. Many magazines like short, snappy pieces and have a wide variety of them in each issue. Others prefer a lengthier, more detailed article, with a more factual and informative slant. It's up to you during your market study to tailor each article to the needs of each particular magazine.

I have already mentioned the *Writers' & Artists' Yearbook* as a source of markets and you can certainly cut down your outlay on magazines by looking up the most usual length of articles in this useful book. But nothing takes the place of reading several current issues of a particular publication, absorbing the flavour of it and getting to know the likes and dislikes of the editorial brain, which will soon become apparent to you.

Contributors' Bulletin published by Arthur Waite in Manchester deals with markets of all descriptions, and is a worthwhile publication for the article writer.

Making the most of your material

Once you find a good subject to write about, you can use your basic research many times, tailoring your article to a variety of magazines. Obviously, each approach would be different. You might use a tongue-in-cheek title for a weekend paper, while a more serious magazine would expect a weightier title, and the content would follow the same pattern.

As an example of what I mean, take as the subject of an article "The Art of Cooking in a Microwave Oven". To me, that bald statement would be uninspiring, unless I was a serious cookery student and wanted to find out the basic facts with no frills. The article that followed should therefore be written in the same informative and no-nonsense style. "Me and my Microwave" conjures up a totally different image, yet the content could be almost the same, written in a much more lighthearted way. How about "No Dear, I meant a Microwave, not a Permanent Wave . . ." immediately I see this article with a comic sketch alongside it, perhaps slanted for a magazine such as *My Weekly*. There are many more ways in which to use the same theme. "The Age of the Micro—Is it Safe?" A possibility for a magazine such as *Good Housekeeping* or *Cosmopolitan*. Still the basic idea for all these articles would be the same: the use of the microwave oven.

Interviewing a prominent or senior local citizen can produce ideas for further articles on how your town has changed over the years, or bring forth hitherto unknown facts about it. Indeed, the person might themselves be a suitable subject. Always get permission first, though, and show your interviewee your finished article before submitting it to the local newspaper. You don't want a libel suit on your hands, or an irate or distressed elderly citizen on your doorstep.

If you write articles about anniversaries, make them unusual ones. Try to ferret out ones that are completely lost in the mists of time, because magazines are inundated with the big four—Christmas, Easter, birthdays and Hallowe'en.

An article-writer becomes a collector. Snippets of useful information in newspapers and magazines are gathered and collated in any way you find most useful to yourself. Mine tend to be filed haphazardly, but that's because I'm not solely an article-writer. My files on local and historical research for my novels are much more orderly!

I do collect brochures—holiday, travel, museum, anything and everything can provide a fund of information for articles and spark you off on something you may never have thought of before. The letters pages of magazines can give you plenty of ideas. Indeed, the writer who can't think of something to write about isn't worth his salt.

Perhaps that's being a little unfair to those who have never written anything before. You think you know nothing, or that what you do know would be of no interest to anyone else. But each person is an individual, and we all have that personal knowledge that is exclusive to us. Your boring job, perhaps. So you pack peanuts? Does everybody? Why not write an amusing article about it?

You're tied to the house with arthritis? If you have ever read a marvellous book entitled *One Step at a Time* by Marie Joseph, you will know how one lady overcomes her disability, and has helped many another sufferer by writing about it. Maybe you could never write a book, but an article might be of immense interest to others.

Your church has a twisted spire and there's a bit of local history about it that you've never really bothered to investigate? The article-writer would seize on this, and either write up all he could about that one church, or do some research and find out if there were any more in the country and write snippets about them all. Such a topic could be sold to various magazines, local and otherwise, written up in different ways.

DIY activities are of enormous interest to people. Years ago my husband and I bought our first touring caravan and did a lot of work on it to make it accommodate our growing family, and to bring it up to date. I wrote up all the detailed alterations that we did, my husband took good clear black-and-white photographs to illustrate the various stages of our work, and I sold the article with photos to a caravan and camping magazine.

Smaller articles I sold to them didn't always warrant photographs, but I did the occasional line-drawing to go with them. Note: always send photos with your articles if it needs them; they will have a much likelier chance of publication. The photos needn't be enormous, postcard size will do. Clarity is the important thing.

While on the subject of photography, we used to take a lot of colour slides, and have sold quite a number of them to magazines to use as illustrations, usually submitted with a small text, to be used or not at the magazine's discretion. Such slides could be tried on travel brochures, county magazines, or postcard manufacturers. Often, local outlets will use them. Those that bought our slides copied the originals, and returned them to us.

A writer carries a notebook at all times. (Or that's the noble intention—I frequently forget mine and have to cram information on old grocery bills.) I would advise you to carry a notebook! Even in the house when you're doing some ordinary job, inspiration may suddenly come to you, and it pays to jot down the bare bones of an idea while it's fresh in your mind.

Even if you only wrote "MicroWave—Pros and Cons", because you happened to be juggling with two dishes of vegetables that wouldn't fit into your device, you'd be instantly reminded of your idea when you picked up the piece of paper again. All too often, an idea is as ephemeral as a summer breeze. Once it's lost, it can be lost forever.

If you have a brilliant idea for a series of articles, by all means write to a magazine of your choice with your suggestions. Back them up with a sample article and titles of future offerings. Send a stamped-addressed envelope—this goes for *all* submissions—or at least a stamp to cover return postage should it be necessary, and await developments.

Structuring your article

Every kind of published writing consists of three important parts: a beginning, a middle and an end. Of course, this is obvious. What may not be so obvious to the beginner however, is how important each of those elements really are.

The title has already been mentioned. This is the bait to lure the reader on to the author's hook. An article may be no more than 500 words in length, so it must then get to the point as quickly as possible with that all-important first paragraph. This is the one that the readers will scan, and which will either grab their interest or tell them very positively that they can't be bothered to read all that stuff.

Your first paragraph *must* interest the reader. A simple statement of what it is all about may be all that's necessary. Beginning with a question is often a good lead-in. The reader will be mentally answering the question and will want to know whether the author agrees with them or not (and will feel satisfyingly smug if the author does or argumentative if he/she doesn't. Either way, the reader has been drawn into the article).

A slightly controversial beginning is a useful opener but get those facts in, quick and punchy, and don't let your reader's attention wander. Don't make that first paragraph too long. Remember that you're still enticing your reader to go on reading. Later paragraphs can expand your theme still more, but don't let up on the information you're imparting.

An article with a good first paragraph and a cleverly worded finale is your aim. But without a substantial middle section to support the others, the result will be like a cake that's sunk in the middle.

So when you think about the article you're going to write, be sure that you have something to say. Construct it well, and write about something that interests *you*—the chances are that it will also interest somebody else.

The following is a small summary of the kind of articles that don't stand much chance of getting into print.

> Articles told in diary-style, consisting of no more than the writer's daily doings, which will be of no interest to anyone else. (Even your best beloved will probably be bored with it.)

> Articles sent to the wrong market. Be prepared to work at this craft of writing—others do it, so can you.

> Articles that are pedantic and dull; so full of pomposity that they read more like sermons.

> Articles that are obviously cruel and racist.

> Articles applauding cruelty to animals, e.g. battery hens. Britain is a nation of animal-lovers.

> Articles that are really reports.

> Articles that waffle, and are merely a sounding-board for the writer, having no real knowledge to impart to the reader.

> Articles that are boring.

But you would write none of those, would you? If so, please go back to the beginning of the chapter and start again.

4

From A to Z

Oh no, I hear you groan. Can't we get to something more interesting? And what exactly is this heading supposed to mean? Be patient a minute.

Except for the very fortunate few, every writer has rejections at some stage or other, so you might as well get used to the idea right now. It's a fine and wonderful thing to get an idea for an article, story or novel, to write it up and think that you've done with it—pack it up, send it off to an agent or publisher, sit back and wait for Things To Happen.

What will probably happen, unless you're very lucky indeed, is that your masterpiece will come hurtling back to you with the speed of an express train. You'll be utterly devastated and wonder just what went wrong. Well, probably nothing, except that you didn't give yourself enough time to give your work the extra bit of attention that it deserves.

I'm not going to tell you to polish it, because it's a description of writing that I particularly hate. You may read it in other manuals. Polish and polish your work until it becomes a little gem . . . ugh. I find that phrase as twee as a million others that you will learn to avoid in your writing apprenticeship. The sentiments may be the same, but the choice of words in any piece of writing is of immense importance to you and your readers, and some that you think are terrific may grate on them. So let's begin again.

The vision was the idea that you thought was so spectacular you couldn't wait to get it down on paper. The revision comes with the second (or third or fourth) reading when you discover that it isn't quite so spectacular after all, and there are things that need to be changed, altered, scratched out and come to

32

terms with. Some things may need very little revision, just a word changed here and there, so don't be inhibited by the thought that you must change everything you first thought of to make it saleable.

It would be impossible to underline every conceivable fault that could lie in anyone's writing. It would undoubtedly be so demoralizing that no beginner would ever dare submit anything ever again. I wouldn't be so presumptuous as to think I knew every mistake, anyway. (If so, I wouldn't still be making them.)

Instead, I've compiled an A to Z list that touches on the most common writing areas in which faults occur, the things to watch out for in doing that all-essential revision, or simply the occasional word that is part of a writer's vocabulary. These can concern experienced writers and beginners alike, so don't ever think you're alone with your writing problems.

There was a vast choice of words I could have used in the following compilation and you may feel that many different words are more suitable. I hope you do. It will show that your writing muscle is getting to work. Here are a few to get you thinking; two for the price of each letter.

AFFECTATION. The use of flowery words and phrases, resulting in stilted dialogue and long-winded descriptions. Try to write as visually as possible, so that your reader sees your scenes as you see them in your head. This will help to avoid the duplication of sentences all trying to describe the same thing.

ARROGANCE. In fictional romantic heroes, it's old hat. Men who are strong and masterful and with the charisma to make the heroine fall in love with them, do not have to be arrogant and objectionable. Arrogance in yourself as an author is best avoided at all time. Nobody loves a bragger, and the old saying goes "you're only as good as your last book".

BOREDOM. Being boring in anything you write means certain failure. The boredom factor may vary slightly in your reading audience, but always give them credit for being intelligent. Don't baby your readers or blind them with science. Be interesting.

33

BACKGROUND. Whatever kind of fiction you write, give your characters a substantial background in which to exist. Don't let them live in a void, appearing as if by magic or immaculate conception, with no family, friends, scenic surroundings or occupational direction.

CHARACTERIZATION. Make it as believable as possible. Readers must really feel that the people in your book existed. Even though they know perfectly well they came out of the author's imagination, the essence of a good storyteller is to create the illusion that the characters in the book live and breathe.

CLICHÉS. Avoid wherever possible. Sometimes you will want a character to be recognized by his or her use of clichés, which is perfectly valid. But in the prose sequences, don't rely on tired old phrases because you're too lazy to think up something original.

DETAIL. Enough is enough. A historical novel that gives endless amounts of detail can stop being fascinating and become boring. Know when to stop by reading published works of the type you want to write. Filter in detail so that it becomes part of the story but does not swamp it.

DIALOGUE. People must speak to one another in fiction. You can't avoid it, however much it bothers you to write it. Practise your dialogue out loud on a tape recorder or in the bath. Best of all, put yourself in the role of your characters and listen to their voices as you write; then your dialogue will be as they would say it.

ESCAPISM. Your job as a storyteller of fiction is to transport readers to another time and place, apart from the ordinary mundane world in which he or she lives. As a factual writer, your aim is the same, within the bounds of the article or book that you are writing. All writing is a form of escape for the reader—let it be enjoyed.

ESSAYS. An essay is what you wrote in school. It is not a short story, an article, a novel or a poem.

FANTASY. Don't make your novel so unbelievable that it stretches the imagination too far (unless you're writing science-fiction). Allow your readers into their escape route from reality, but don't turn your story into a farce.

FLASHBACKS. In novel-writing, this is a useful way of letting the reader know about something essential that happened in the character's past. Never be tempted to tell a whole novel in flashback, telling the reader on the last page that it was all a dream, anyway. TV soap operas may get away with it—once. You never would.

GREMLINS. The nasty little bugs that turn writing days into mental blocks, when nothing goes right and you're convinced you'll never be able to write again. This is when you're tempted to forget the whole thing. Do just that—for a little while. Take the day off. Do something entirely different. Your mind will be refreshed when you think that you might *just* have another go, and the ideas will come surging (or trickling) back.

GUIDELINES. Some magazines and publishers will send guidelines on request, outlining their needs. Study them but don't follow them slavishly or the publications will be receiving identical work from you and everyone else, and none of you will be published. The best guidelines are in your own head, using your own instincts through market study and common sense.

HESITATION. He who hesitates is lost. (An example of a cliché). So you've finished your article/story/novel, done your revision to the best of your ability, and now you suddenly worry about what the family will think. Or you're sure it's not good enough. Or the editor will issue a writ for defamation of character in your historical saga . . . rubbish. You're just getting cold feet, to use another cliché, and no manuscript ever got published until it was offered to an editor. If you spent all those hours writing it, give it the respect it deserves and send it off.

HOPE. Every writer needs it. Don't lose it when that horrible plopping sound of your returned manuscript hitting the doormat drags you down. Tomorrow's post may be better, but not unless you have several items written and sent out. Always having another option will soften the blow of a rejection.

IMAGINATION. Lack of it may mean you're best suited to writing factual works, and I'm not denigrating them in the least. To be a successful fiction-writer, you *must* have some imagination and be able to use it. To see the world as your characters see it is vital: it's their story you're telling, not yours.

INCOME TAX. Everyone's least favourite subject. But when you begin to earn money from your writing, you must declare it to the tax collector. Refer to the *Writers' & Artists' Yearbook* for more detailed information on this subject. If you become prolific, you will benefit from the services of an accountant. If rich, VAT will figure in your life. . . .

JOY. This is a sneaky one, because it really means enjoyment. If you don't enjoy what you write, then it's unlikely that anyone else will enjoy it. I don't need to add any more to that, do I?

JAM on the bread. All the peripheral activities you will be involved in when your name becomes known. It's fun to be recognized and makes all the hours of solitary writing even more worthwhile. But more of that later.

KISSING (Mainly for romantic novelists). Watch how you describe that kiss. The romantic genre is often maligned, and much of it is due to the slushy descriptions of kissing. Lips do not plunder, nor do many heroines wish to be bruised. Ears do not have to be nibbled to convey tenderness, nor fingers caressed and half-eaten. Regency novelists can convey passion with a touch of the lover's lips on the gloved hands, so don't overdo it.

KEEN. All writers have a keen mind; they become intensely interested in everything around them. Writers stay young, which is a bonus many people don't realize until they begin writing. A writer's brain cannot remain stagnant—while there is something to write about, they will write.

LOVE SCENES. Unavoidable in romantic novels, otherwise write something else. They should be tender, always romantic, occurring at inevitable moments in the book and never thrown in because you think the editor will want to see one about now. They can be explicit or gentle, to suit the mood of the book, and if you are unsure how to write them, should be studied in successful novels.

LESS THAN PERFECT. You will feel you are this many times. You tread a fine line between confidence and diffidence. No one is perfect, or would want to be. No piece of writing is without faults, even from the most professional of published writers. How many books or articles have you read where you dispute a sentence? All you can do is your best.

METAPHORS. As with similes, try to invent your own, make them intelligent and witty, and editors will love you. Overdone similes come into the same category as clichés and can quickly become tedious to read. Original writing is a pleasure to read, to editors and readers alike.

MULTIPLE SUBMISSIONS. Sounds alarming, doesn't it? What it means is sending the same piece of writing to various editors or publishers at the same time. Feature-editors hate it. Publishers used to, but some authors and agents are now doing this with book manuscripts. It certainly saves time, but be prepared to get six rejections back in one day instead of one.

NAMES. In fiction the names you choose for each of your characters should suit their personality, status, background and the era in which you set your book. Don't have a Wayne in an Edwardian novel, or call your scullery maid Clarissa. Give your main characters the most likeable names, but avoid letting the names of your villains be too obviously scurrilous.

NEVER ON SUNDAY. Some writers have only limited time in which to write, and feel guilty at "deserting" their families while they shut themselves away in a cupboard to scribble. Much of the writing that you do is done in the head before it's even transmitted to paper. Even while walking the children to the park or cooking the Sunday roast, planning your work can still go on in your head. You may forget some of it (unless you have your notebook handy) but something will be retained for when you get to your own space. Or just take Sunday off.

OPTIMISM. Write everything in this frame of mind and it will show through. Believe that everything is possible and some of it will be. Don't get knocked down by the first rejection: pick yourself up and start again. Many famous authors survived dozens of rejections before making the breakthrough. So can you, if you believe in yourself and have the will to succeed.

OPENING. Your gateway to the splendid piece of writing you want someone else to read. Make it attractive and welcoming enough to let the reader in. No matter how small the piece, or how magnificent the saga, the opening is what your reader sees first. Don't let him be disappointed.

PADDING. If two words will make your point perfectly, don't labour on for several sentences, saying the same thing in different ways. Waffling won't disguise a badly constructed story that is really no more than a brief incident. You may think you can get away with it but editors will see through it in a moment, and it will be rejection time again.

PACE. The way in which any piece of writing is handled by the author. A snappy little article needs to breeze along. A historical saga can be more leisurely. Pace can also influence the *balance* of your writing. For instance, don't rush into the first 20 pages of a novel, and leave nothing to say for the next 250.

QUOTATIONS. Can be extremely helpful when the mind is blank and you cannot find that elusive title. Reversing a well-known quotation can make a witty title for an article, and a book of quotations is a useful addition to any writer's bookshelf.

QUIET. What writers need in order to write . . . or do they? It all depends on the individual. Write to pop music if it suits you, or traffic noises if you have to. But don't use the lack of quiet as an excuse not to write!

READING. While you're developing writing skills, read other people's work. Learn to read novels with a writer's eye as well as for pleasure. Find the key points in any article and see how it was constructed. Market study is there for the taking, on every library shelf, in every paperback store, in any magazine or newspaper. Addresses of each one are on the editorial page, so there are no excuses for not knowing where to send your work.

READERS. Without them, there would be no point in writing for publication. They are as necessary to us as our pens and typewriters. Nothing compares with the glow of a reader telling you how much he enjoyed your latest book/article, etc. Never disappoint readers who send you fan letters, and never be too busy or important to talk to them when you meet them in person.

SUSPENSE. This can be defined in different ways for any kind of writing that you do, and is essential in one form or another for all. Keep them guessing when you can. Make them want to turn that page or read on to the end of the story or article. Don't give away everything that you want to say in the first few sentences.

STYLE. This is all your own; unique to you. I was once asked during a television interview if I saw myself as a second —— ———. "No," I answered. "I don't want to be a second anybody." I wasn't being arrogant, just truthful. Who really wants their writing to be likened to someone else's? It may be intended to be flattering, but it's far better to be known for your own individual style.

TALENT. Yes, it takes talent to put any piece of writing together, and talent is inborn. But many of us don't realize our potential in any field until we give it a try. Who was born knowing that they were a writer? Until you put those first words onto paper, you have no idea how eloquent you can be. Somebody, somewhere, might be dying to read those words you're about to write.

TOUGHNESS. Even the fluffiest successful lady-writer is undoubtedly tougher than you might think. The writer who gives up at the first setback will never know the heady delight of being told that their manuscript has been accepted, or the very personal and exclusive pleasure of holding that first published book in their hand. Isn't it worth a few disappointments to reach that eventual goal?

UNDERSTANDING. Of human nature in particular. A writer has to be something of a sociologist in order to know what makes people tick. Putting together a cast of characters and giving each one individual personalities is not the easiest thing in the world. And this is only a small part of the fiction-writer's task. Settings, conflict, authenticity, research, construction, a story with a beginning, middle and an end, all play their part. Understand all that too, and you have some insight into the intricacies of a writer's life.

UNUSUAL. In non-fiction of any kind, always look for the unusual subject, or the unusual angle to write about. Editors who have been in the publishing business for many years will fall upon the writer who can give them freshness and vitality in their scripts.

VISUAL. The kind of writing that lifts a story from the mundane into the truly beautiful. See that glorious sunset and describe what you see, so that the reader sees it too. Taste as well as feel the heat in the desert, and convey that feeling to your reader. Know the touch of a dry autumn leaf, and let the reader know its touch and its beauty by painting pictures with your words.

VOICE. Write with your own, and nobody else's. Don't copy other writers' pet phrases. In fiction, endow each of your characters with a voice of their own, because it's an essential human element by which each of us is recognizably different. It is just as important in fiction as in real life.

WRITING. The sheer physical and mental work that goes into any work of fiction or non-fiction. Don't let anyone tell you it's easy but don't be put off by the daunting thought of having to write so many thousand words a day because a manual tells you so. It's your life. Use it how you will. If your choice is to write, and other writers' words can be of help, be guided by them—but not to the extent of following them blindly.

WORDS. Without them, no piece of writing ever got produced. Use the most emotive ones you can to express a point, and don't be sloppy in your writing. The next article an editor reads might have been written with more care than yours, and guess which one will be published?

XYLONITE. There, you see? You've just learned a new word. It's a kind of celluloid, a compound used instead of ivory. Who said a writer didn't expand her knowledge in the course of trying to find a word beginning with X?

EXCITEMENT. Yes, now I'm cheating. While you don't necessarily want to give your readers heart attacks by filling every page with exciting happenings, neither do they want to be sent to sleep by the same old dum-de-dum storyline. Characters who have everything going right for them do not fill the requirements of novels. Characters whose lives are thrown into conflict by the plot or their relationships are the stuff of which novels are made.

YELLOW. Not the cowardly kind, but the clear citrus shade of lemons, or the brilliance of sunlight in a summer sky. Wouldn't you find those descriptions more evocative than plain boring old yellow? This is the place where a bit of descriptive writing enhances your story.

YOU. I devour books like these, because however long you have been writing, you are always learning. You can always pick up tips from other writers but, in the end, you have to do the writing. No one else can do it for you. So don't even use a how-to book as an excuse to put off that moment you sit down and begin.

ZEAL. The industry you put into all your writing. Apply yourself and hopefully all your hard work will pay you back dividends. They may be modest at first, but one of the joys of a writer's life is that you never know what's just around the corner.

ZODIAC. No, I'm not referring to your birth sign, but using a roundabout way of saying that you too could reach the stars. In writing terms, anything is possible.

5

Short Stories

Everyone knows what a short story is, but just as I defined what an article was not, I am also going to define what a short story is not. It is not a condensed novel. It is not an anecdote, a string of witty pieces of dialogue held together by the flimsiest of plots, and neither is it an essay or a report. The ideal short story, that will please an editor, has a sharp crisp beginning to catch the reader's interest, a well-constructed middle to hold that interest and a conclusive ending to satisfy the reader.

Are you now thinking you've read something like that before? Yes, you have. The construction of every piece of writing has similarities. Far from making you cross because you think I'm covering the same ground again, I hope it gives you some comfort in knowing that simple fact.

But construction is only one part of short-story writing. I'm going to deal with the ending first. This may seem odd to you, but the type of story you are writing will often dictate the ending. The ending can be sad or funny, romantic or with a twist in the tail. Whatever kind of ending you use, let it fit the rest of your story, and make it logical to the plot. Nothing annoys an editor more than being led up the garden path in a story. Let the reader be misled or confused during the relating of your story if you must—as long as the ending is then perfectly logical, and they can look back and see that everything pointed to your conclusion after all.

Markets for short stories have shrunk considerably in recent years. Many of the magazines that published mine have gone: *Sunday Companion, Red Star Weekly, Favourite Story, New Love, Love Affair, True Story* and *Hers*, to name but a few. Those that are left therefore have all those story-writers competing for space in their magazines, which tells you the same old thing—you have to be good to be published.

The short story is a wish-fulfilment for the reader, and since the majority of short stories are written for women, I will refer to the reader as female. In the space of time it takes her to read a short story—under the dryer at the hairdresser's, having a quick cup of coffee before fetching the children from school—she can be transported away from worries about mortgages, school uniforms and meeting her husband's boss. The short story will take her away to unknown places, exotic or amusing. While she reads of it she can dream of being someone else. She can indulge in a secondhand love affair, or visit some new and glamorous location in her imagination.

Market study is essential for short-story writing. Read the magazines of your choice, and get to know the format the editor likes. I did detailed market study when I first began writing short stories, analysing the magazines thoroughly. Not only the number of words required but lengths of sentences, paragraphs, balance of dialogue to plot, etc. This was my rough guide and, although I didn't follow every conclusion avidly, it made sense not to offer a one-page story to a magazine that liked 5–6,000-word pieces concerning fairly serious topics.

Tell your story with a certain simplicity and an economic use of words. One situation or problem for the characters is often enough for the reader to cope with, without any little side-plots that confuse and become an irritation. Your reader can only learn a certain amount about the characters in several thousand words, and won't want to be wasting her time with reading trivia that adds nothing to the story.

So avoid those unnecessary details. Let's take as an example the family problem of whether Grandma should go into an old people's home. This is the theme of your story. Don't go off at a tangent by reminiscing about how different things were 50 years ago. Don't insert a bit of author-cleverness by remarking that Grandma should be glad she's not an eskimo, and then go on to relate at length how the eskimos sent their old people out to die to avoid being a burden to their families. Don't tell five other stories about interesting inmates of the home to which Grandma may be sent. Don't bring in all Matron's problems with the staff, or add an aside about how she'd always wanted to go into musical comedy really, but this paid better . . . it may sound far-fetched, but it's perilously easy to get so enthusiastic about the situation that the writer gets completely diverted from the main storyline.

The more sideline incidents you introduce, the less likelihood there is of your story being accepted. Reading such a story begins to sound like a child's essay, with its continual use of the words "and then", "and then", "and then", until the reader is completely bewildered, and forgets what the story was supposed to be about.

To go back to Grandma and the home . . . this is a story that would be suitable for a variety of markets—it all depends which treatment you decide to give it. *My Weekly, Woman's Story* and *Woman's Realm* are three possibilities. The experienced writer will know that this is a theme that can have every bit of emotion wrung out of it. It could also be a delightfully humorous story, with Grandma a cheerful old stick who has no intention of being put anywhere.

But even if you decide to tackle it humorously, bring in moments of emotion and conflict, otherwise there's no story. As a writer, your aim is to get an emotional reaction from your reader, whether a smile or a tear or a tug at the heart.

If your reader is totally unmoved at the end of your story, you've failed in your bid to entertain her. To get emotion out of a story, be prepared to put some in. Forget Auntie's disapproving look and learn to write with emotion and sincerity.

One last bit of advice about Grandma's story. Most beginners would tell this story from the anxious daughter's viewpoint. Fine, if you can find a new twist, but it's been done many times before. Try telling the story from Grandma's viewpoint, or that of a teenage granddaughter's or small child. You can often pep up a well-used theme by using a narrator that the reader wouldn't expect.

Finding ideas

How do you find ideas for short stories? As with articles, ideas can come from many sources. Often it's a TV programme that triggers the idea, or problem pages in magazines. It may be a

44

photograph, or the little editorial blurb beneath a published story that you can use to think up an entirely new plot. Read the blurb, but not the published story, and you'll be surprised at the new idea the blurb will evoke.

When you've got the idea, ask yourself some questions and jot down the answers as they occur to you. Suppose you decide to have two characters stuck in a snowbound hotel for a weekend. Ask yourself about them. Who are they? Why are they there? Did they arrive together? Are they strangers/lovers/sworn enemies? What difference will their meeting make to their lives? What time of day/year is it? Is that significant to these two people?

By the time you've written down such questions and answers, and any more that occur to you, you should be building up a picture of the characters and the background in which you're putting them. You should know their names and their relationship, and you should have decided what you're trying to tell the reader about them—that is, their problem, and how they're going to resolve it.

I used this story in an issue of *Hers*. My couple were divorced. The man had since re-married, but the ex-wife wanted him back and made sure she was at the hotel which she knew he habitually stayed at on business trips. They had once spent a weekend at this hotel, which brought nostalgia into the story.

The original idea often changes as the story evolves in a writer's mind, and my hotel wasn't snowbound in the end, but the roads approaching it became impassable due to heavy rain, and people staying at the hotel were advised not to travel unless absolutely necessary. This was, frankly, a contrived situation, but worked out in such a way that it was perfectly logical.

Note that using weather conditions is a useful way of helping matters along.

For this story it was easy to find a beginning with impact, told by the ex-wife as narrator, watching for a familiar car to approach through the wet country roads. In the first important paragraph, I conveyed her anxiety, location, and weather conditions. All these were pointers to the reader, although she wouldn't recognize them as such at that stage.

Give your reader little clues throughout, so you don't have to suddenly bring out a mass of facts on the last page, explaining all.

This story continued with the shock of the husband finding the ex-wife there at the hotel; his initial annoyance, gradual feeling of attraction, and eventual rejection of her because of his loyalties to his new wife. Then came the narrator's realization that the love they once had really was all over and could never be revived, and finally her decision to come to terms with it all. A potentially downbeat ending could then be one of hope for the future.

Structure

Although it's important to hook your reader with the first few sentences, don't then bombard her with everything at once. In real life, we learn about people gradually, and your story should unfold in the same way, revealing a little more with each scene. I always think in scenes when I write. In a short story, one long scene with no change of pace or setting would be deadly dull; too many scene changes would be like the rush-hour at Victoria Station.

When you're analysing short stories, notice the scenes the writers use, and the transition from one to the next, sometimes smooth and sometimes startling, to suit the story. Writing is such a flexible and personal craft that there are many ways of blending the techniques and this is one of the things that makes it continually fascinating.

A short story is invariably told from one narrator's viewpoint: there isn't room, as there is in the novel, to enter into different characters' heads. Keeping to one person's viewpoint also means that everything you write will be sharply illuminated from his or her mind. Writing in the first or third person will depend on your story and your market.

What the narrator thinks, feels, sees and hears, must be the most important facets of the story; avoid author intrusion at all time. This can sometimes happen without being realized, maybe

46

by a couple of sentences appearing in the present tense as if the author has inserted a little aside in the manner of an old-time drama; or a bit of home-spun philosophy is put in to prove a point, adding nothing to the plot, and only succeeding in irritating the editor who reads it. Of course, if it's the *character* who does the bit of moralizing, that's entirely different.

In a short story, your aim is to select the most important and interesting facts about characters and situation and to concentrate on them. Give the reader enough to work on and let her supply the rest with her own imagination. In other words, don't feel the necessity to explain everything in painful detail as if you're talking to a child.

If you say that your character lifted the weight of her hair from her neck and walked along the street with her transistor held close to her ear, it's hardly necessary to say that she's a teenager with long hair as well. Feed in the information through the story and be as professional as you can by using implication rather than a mass of stark statements.

Give your characters a problem to solve. Don't make the solution glaringly obvious from page one. Let your characters have human failings and quirks. Make your plots interesting. Make them come alive on the pages, and be sure you care about your own characters and their problems because, if you don't, neither will anybody else. Short stories move along quite quickly, but don't usually cover a long period of time. The most successful short stories have a sense of immediacy about them; a story that covers a period of years is usually best kept for a novel.

If you're just thinking about writing short stories, you may have trouble in getting as much as the germ of an idea, even from such reliable sources as I've mentioned. It may comfort you to know that you will gradually develop a "plot mind", but it helps to develop this by jotting things down as they occur to you, just as in article-writing.

The following is a summary of the questions you should be asking yourself while you're writing your short story.

● Will the title catch the reader's eye, and put the reader in the right mood for the kind of story you're writing?

Some magazines will change your title, but you should still give it the best label you can. It's the first thing that the editor will see and you must make him or her want to read it.

● Does the opening of the story interest the reader by taking her quickly to an interesting character, incident or setting?

It doesn't matter whether it's a crisp piece of dialogue or a descriptive sentence or two, as long as it catches the reader's attention and makes her want to read on.

● Can the beginning of the story be easily understood by a reader with no previous knowledge of your plot and characters?

By this, I mean that you musn't be obscure in your opening scene. You're sharing an experience with your reader, so let her in on the action.

● Is the problem in the story made clear and interesting in the first scene?

Not quite the same as the previous question. The problem may not be in the first few sentences, but should certainly be in the first scene.

● Are you convinced that all the action is feasible?
If you're not, neither will the reader be.

● Every incident should develop out of the one before it. Does it? And does the suspense increase gradually?

Not necessarily the Alfred Hitchcock type of suspense, but the question that you put in the reader's mind as to the outcome of the story. Without this, she'll be bored.

● Have you included side-issues that have nothing to do with the story?

If so, cut them out. Be ruthless. The central problem must be important enough for the reader to enjoy seeing how the characters resolve it.

● Have you created one attractive, central character with whom the reader can identify or sympathize?

48

There must be one central character in a short story, so make him or her the most important one, the one around whom the story revolves.

● Does your character speak with dialogue applicable to his or her age, status, personality, locality?

Self-explanatory, and dialogue will be covered in detail in a later chapter.

● Does your story end satisfactorily, and not depending on coincidence and farcical situations?

Don't ruin a good story by the use of a device. Coincidences happen in real life, rarely in fiction. Anyway, readers feel cheated and are left with a sense of let-down if the characters haven't solved their problems logically.

Confession stories

In any kind of fiction, the drama is slightly larger than life. However simple a story may look, the writer must work hard to achieve that effect. The confession or true-life story may look the easiest of all to write, relying heavily on emotional situation as it does; in reality it is the hardest to get right. If this is what you want to try, for magazines such as *Loving* or *Woman's Story*, then strong characterization and uninhibited writing are the basic requirements—always in the first person, of course.

Confession stories are often maligned, because people imagine they consist of sex and sin and not much else. Read the published stories and you may be surprised at the range they use, often dealing with social problems and less usual aspects of life.

When you write a confession story for the first time, try to imagine yourself in the role of the heroine confiding everything to her best friend. Tell her what you're burning to confess and tell it in everyday language, not in stilted phrases; have a good dramatic story to tell, because that's what the readers of these stories expect.

There's an art to confession-story writing, but it can be

learned. The main fault in the new writer is in being too literary. This is not how you would talk to your closest confidante, so keep that thought in mind. The plots may be too artificial. Remember that readers of these stories, more than any others, are looking for characters with whom they can identify. It's the kind of story that makes them think that "there, but for the grace of God, go I".

Contrary to popular belief—and always voiced by people who have never read confession stories—there is a definite moral tone about them. The old adage of sex, sin and repent may apply to some of them but, however explicit it may be, the central character always sees her wrong-doing in time, and faces the future as a wiser person.

Always give your characters motivation for their actions. Always give them some conflict to resolve. This applies to all short stories, and to all fiction.

Dialogue and characterization are also common to all fiction, and will be dealt with in the following chapter.

Finally, some imaginary editorial comments on seeing a pile of short stories on the desk on a wet Monday morning, after a heavy weekend and a domestic row before leaving home. (Yes, editors have other lives too.)

"Throw this out. Why do they send in five-thousand word stories when we only publish two-thousand max?"

"A supernatural story for a serious gardening magazine?"

"Listen to this beginning, Sue or Jane or Bill. 'The story I am about to relate takes place in the mythical country of Supervania . . . *out!*"

"Here's a beauty. 'My dog's first lady-friend was call Betty, which was also the name of my Granny, which we all thought was a funny coincidence.' Etc, etc."

"'The sun *hemmoraged* across the sky.' Anyone for jam doughnuts this morning? The guy can't spell, either."

"This one can't afford a new typewriter ribbon, and I can't waste time deciphering it."

"Stories? Since when did we start publishing stories?"

By now, the editor will be throwing out all but the neatest manuscripts, with the word-count clearly displayed on the title page; those stories that fit the content of the magazine, and which grab the editor's attention at once as being suitable for publication. The rest will be sent back; those with SAEs getting prior attention, those without may not be sent back at all. It all depends on the editor. But initially, it all depends on you.

6

Characters and Dialogue

A story without people in it is like an unfinished symphony: beautiful but incomplete, or not so beautiful and boring. Characters bring any scene to life and yet, for many writers, the creating of a fictitious being that is exclusive to their imagination is completely beyond them.

Before I go more deeply into how you make these characters more believable, read the sentences below.

> Lucy trudged along the street.
> Lucy skipped along the street.
> Lucy walked dreamily along the street.
> Lucy tip-toed along the street.
> Lucy wandered along the street.

Five very short sentences using the same Christian name and the same location yet, by the use of one more word (in sentence three, there were two) the reader is left with an instant idea of Lucy. Still perplexed? Look at the choice of verb again and the following analysis.

Lucy *trudged* might suggest an elderly woman or a housewife loaded down with shopping bags.

Lucy *skipped* would most likely refer to a child.

Lucy who *walked dreamily* is obviously in love.

Lucy *tip-toed* because it was dark, or she was nervous, or she was creeping up on somebody. Whichever meaning you have chosen, this would intrigue the reader.

Lucy who *wandered* could be a child again, or a bored teenager or an older person with time to waste.

If you used any one of these sentences as the beginning of a story, the use of the verb in all cases would stimulate the reader's imagination at the outset, so that they wonder *why* Lucy moved in that particular way. And once you've put that question in the reader's mind and captured their interest, they'll read on. With one short sentence, the use of the character's name and one verb, you've intrigued your reader. Not so difficult, was it?

Having got that far, be sure to let your story be motivated by that one qualifying word. There must be a reason for Lucy to walk the way she did and this must form part of the plot. Don't cheat the reader by planting an intrigue that you can't follow through.

Sometimes it's difficult for a beginner to write that all-important first sentence and first scene. My advice is to get on with the story and write the beginning later. By then, your mind will be filled with what you want to say, and that essential crisp beginning will come to you all the more easily. A neat little sentence like one of those above is the simplest and yet one of the most effective scene-setters.

Still with Lucy . . . perhaps your story is going to be about an old lady having the chance to visit relatives in Australia and being nervous at the thought of flying. You've written the story, but the beginning meanders too much. You might then consider an emotive little sentence like "Lucy trudged along the street."

The question in any reader's mind is "Why?" And you have the story ready and waiting to give the answer.

You have brought Lucy and her feelings immediately into focus by indirect description. You haven't yet told the reader why she's trudging but, as the story unfolds, the reader will be in sympathy with Lucy and know why she was reacting in that way. The reader will have an emotional reaction to the character's problem because you've sown the seeds right at the beginning of the story.

Making your characters real

For your reader to get that emotional reaction, the writer must have one first. As you create your characters, try to feel every bit of anger, sorrow, happiness, love, that they are going to feel in your story. Sympathize with and understand them.

Try to have a visual image of each character that you create. It's easy enough to jot down their physical appearances and any pecularities in dress, mannerisms and so on. But be careful of making them into caricatures in order to establish their looks and personalities. If you find it difficult to visualize an imaginary person, cut out photographs from magazines and describe them as if they were your characters.

Avoid writing about stereotyped characters—not all secretaries are tough cookies with red talons for fingernails, not all Western heroes look like Gary Cooper in High Noon. How many Doctor Spocks can you write about? One pointed-eared hero is enough for any one. Don't make every detective have a dim-witted side-kick, or every cop be bored and tired with a wife who doesn't understand or has recently died, leaving him with a huge chip on his shoulder.

You will create believable characters if you let them grow out of their surroundings and circumstances. Give them an interesting situation and problem so that the reader will care about what is going to happen to them right from the outset. If you wait until the last page to bring up some fascinating fact that Explains All, you'll have lost your reader long ago.

Involve your reader from the beginning. By the end of the story, they will then feel a sense of satisfaction that the characters, whom they too will have come to know, have solved their problems and are going to live happily on beyond the printed page.

Dialogue

Your characters must come alive for the reader. So how on earth do you achieve that? You can describe their appearance, their relationships, occupations, temperament, but they won't really live for the reader until you hear them speak. That dreaded word dialogue must come into your story sooner or later and, in a short story, the sooner the better.

You can look at the most beautiful girl in the world and envy her looks—but if she speaks to you in a voice like a rusty tin can, you can be put off immediately. The voice gives a clue to character—think of the late Richard Burton's rich, warm tones, or the lilting huskiness of Dana.

A page of good dialogue can do more for your story than pages of dense prose. It is not merely a means of breaking up the page so that it looks pretty. Interspersed with descriptive passages, the reader is kept constantly entertained and aware of the movement of the story, instead of it seeming totally static.

Dialogue in fiction serves distinct purposes: sprinkled between passages of prose it reveals character; it develops the plot; it tells readers what happened before the story opened by allowing the characters themselves to discuss the past; and it shows the character's mood at the time of speaking.

An example of this is in the fictional scene below.

"You mean you want me to become a company wife again!"

Frances could hear her own voice, shrill, disbelieving and furious. David's face was suddenly very controlled. She couldn't read his expression. He was remote from her, when she thought they had been on the brink of recapturing the old closeness. . . .

"You're twisting my words as usual," he countered. "I'm asking you to come to London with me as my wife for the duration of the conference. We're still married, Frances, despite this farcical separation."

"We're still separated," she muttered.

He went on as though she hadn't spoken, ruthless as ever.

"After last night, can you still deny there's something between us?"

"After last night," she said bitterly, ignoring the catch in her throat, "I know you haven't changed at all. You think that sex solves everything. And you're still putting the needs of the company above everything else."

The situation between the two characters should need no further explanation. A great deal has been told about them in this short scene. It could come near the beginning of a novel, opening up the conflict between David and Frances and conveying suspense as to how they will resolve their marital and personality problems. Much of the information imparted to the reader came through the dialogue, revealing their present circumstances and mood, something of their past, and the crisis point reached regarding their future.

A more detailed analysis in the way a new writer would dissect the scene is as follows:

"You mean you want me to become a company wife again!"

The reader knows that this is a married couple with some dissension between them. She doesn't yet know if they are divorced or separated or merely having a breakfast-time wrangle.

The next paragraph outlines the irritation more clearly, and suggests the differing temperaments of the two. Frances is volatile at that moment, David capable of keeping his emotions under control in the macho role of the dominant male character. A hint of the sexual attraction still between them is introduced.

"You're twisting my words as usual," he countered. "I'm asking you to come to London with me as my wife for the duration of the conference. We're still married, Frances, despite this farcical separation."

The reader now knows the situation between them. She gleans that Frances is not always tolerant of David, at least in his mind, and that he considers their separation as no more than a hiccup in their relationship, still furthering the image of the macho male, dismissing such female tantrums as of little importance. But to resume a relationship for the sake of a conference gains sympathy for Frances, the main female character, which is the writer's intention.

"We're still separated," she muttered.

The use of the verb is deliberate. If she had stormed at David, the reader would have sensed that there was little chance of Frances going along with his suggestion. But she *mutters*, therefore keeping the voice and the tone of the dialogue low key, suggesting to the reader that she may agree. It's also an indication that she too is not convinced that the separation is permanent.

> He went on as though she hadn't spoken, ruthless as ever.
> "After last night, can you still deny there's something between us?"

David's character is further revealed to the reader. The line of dialogue tells her that they spent the night together. A previous scene may have gone into this in more detail, but if a reader merely picked up this book at random and flipped through the pages, this scene would give her some very definite pointers as to the content.

> "After last night," she said bitterly, ignoring the catch in her throat, "I know you haven't changed at all. You think that sex solves everything. And you're still putting the needs of the company above everything else."

Now we have it. All the innuendo of the previous sentences are stated clearly to the reader. The adverb *bitterly* reveals that Frances is regretting what was probably an inevitable love scene for two passionate characters. The adverb also suggests that she thinks David is only coming back into her life for the good of the company.

The key phrase is *ignoring the catch in her throat*. The reader senses that Frances is far from being unaffected by David, however much she protests, and all the indications now are that she will agree to his suggestion to accompany him at the conference, and eventually their separation will end.

This was a small but emotive scene in a romantic story. It could have been used in a short story or novel. It doesn't waste words or wallow in sentimentality, yet it conveys all the necessary emotions to the reader, and makes them want to read on to see what is going to happen. Much of that questioning in the reader's mind comes through the short sentences of dialogue.

Dialogue reveals character more effectively than a block of prose outlining temperament. As soon as you put those parenthesis marks on the page, you slip into the role of the character who is speaking so, when you write the lines of dialogue, be aware of how that character would say them.

Listen to his or her voice inside your head. Is that sentence precisely how *they* would say it? Don't just put down the first 10 words that come into your head. Write the words that would come into your character's head. If you know this character as you should by now, since they are your creation and yours alone, you should know how they speak, their accent if any, their inflexions, and their emotional reaction to people and situations.

Few people open their mouths and speak in a constant flat monotone. Voices change as people speak. They become faster or slower, rise and fall, and these changing nuances are the ones you should impart in your dialogue. Not always by the use of different adverbs to get away from the dreaded he said/she said business, but by the words you give your characters to say.

Supposing she's young and in love, waiting impatiently for her boyfriend to turn up on the doorstep. Don't let her greet him as if she's 60 years old and welcoming the vicar to tea. If you think this is ridiculous, test your own written dialogue by changing the ages and lifestyles of the characters that you've created.

It should be an impossible exercise. If you used the couple in the previous paragraph or the scene between Frances and David as examples, each set of characters should be so clear-cut in your mind and in your writing, that their dialogue couldn't be anything but that of a young couple in love, or a slightly older couple having problems. So *think* yourself into your characters, and *hear* them as they speak their lines.

Dialogue develops the plot and moves it forward. The characters tell each other, and therefore the reader, of their hopes, fears and joys. They anticipate their anxieties, and so does the reader. They share moments of passion and fury—and so does the reader. Frances and David have shown you that.

Showing the character's mood at the time of writing is one of the most useful aids of dialogue. Adverbs are obvious: she said awkwardly, he spoke softly, she mumbled fearfully.

An active verb is another method of showing the character's mood: he gloated, she wept, he laughed.

Whichever method you use, be sure you convey your exact meaning, or you'll change the reader's appreciation of the sentences very easily. Just as in the earlier examples of Lucy trudging or skipping, Lucy's dialogue can be wrongly interpreted.

"I'm staying home tomorrow," Lucy said angrily.

"I'm staying home tomorrow," Lucy said defiantly.

"I'm staying home tomorrow," Lucy vowed.

"I'm staying home tomorrow," Lucy announced gaily.

"I'm staying home tomorrow," Lucy promised.

"I'm staying home tomorrow," Lucy croaked.

Each of these examples give the reader a different feeling about Lucy's motives for staying home, and only the writer knows which is the correct one. Get it right.

No two people speak exactly alike. Think of your story in a dramatic sense, as if it's a radio play. On radio the actors have to rely solely on dialogue and voice variations; a written story should have as much impact in its characterization.

Although you don't want to wallow in sentimentality, remember that all writing loses something of its initial passion once it's out of your head and written down in cold print. Get the impassioned scene down on paper and then trim it if you really think you've overwritten it.

Always allow your characters to live out their big scenes, whether it's a blistering fight at the ole corral, or a tender tug-of-love. Don't make your scenes too short or they will be over before the reader has become interested in them. In effect, your reader is "eavesdropping" on your characters, and it's more interesting to hear something first-hand this way, than by having the writer reporting the facts. In other words, use plenty of dialogue between the main characters.

Also, make dialogue consistent with the characters you create. If you begin with Frances in her late twenties, don't forget halfway through and give her the dialogue and actions of a 50-year-old. Use the local vocabulary of different professions and lifestyles, but never overdo the use of dialect. This is especially important in a short story where the reader may have only 10 minutes to spare and won't want to decipher North Country phrases or southern slang that cannot be readily understood.

A short story shouldn't be crowded by too many characters. Generally, the shorter the story, the fewer characters and the simpler the storyline. Every extra character you bring in diffuses the importance of the central one.

Make each of your characters strong and make each one an individual—not merely by having a blonde with a brunette sister, but by their personalities. Test your own writing, and other people's, by picking up a story half-read and seeing if you know immediately who is speaking. You should, if the characterization is sound.

It's a mistake to include the character's name in every line of dialogue. It reads very amateurishly, and it shouldn't be necessary if you've distinguished each person as they speak. Give your characters names to suit their personalities and lifestyles.

A character's clothes, too, are an indication of the kind of person he or she is. Don't go on for several pages describing every item a girl is wearing, but a brief mention of someone in a yellow tracksuit, for instance, will conjure up the initial idea of her personality and appearance at once. As would "the bronze, designer cocktail dress worn with the long gilt earrings that Paul had bought her . . . .".

Markets

Finally, a rundown of a diverse selection of short-story markets, with a brief idea of what they will buy. There are many other outlets but if you're interested in this form of writing, you will find them out for yourself. In all cases, the addresses are to be found in the publications.

Woman's Own. Accepts commissioned stories only, except for its annual short-story competition every April.

Sunday Post. Stories of 1,000–2,000 words in length. Strong, human-interest stories, nothing depressing.

My Story. 4,000–5,000 word stories, realistic confession style. Usual characters in the stories are between 20 and 28 years old, married or single.

Woman's Weekly. 2,500–4,500 words. This magazine avoids as themes divorce, politics, racial issues and violence.

Annabel and other D. C. Thomson magazines. Romantic or dramatic stories. Adventure, thrillers, realism, depending on the magazine, which should be studied. A wide variety of stories used. Length, 1,000–4,000 words.

Woman's Realm. Length, 1,000–3,000 words. This magazine has a wide range of fiction and will use the offbeat story. The quality of the writing and the entertainment value are of prime importance.

Woman. 1,500–3,000 words. The age group most generally used in stories is 18–30. General stories, contemporary.

She. Slick, sophisticated stories, often one-pagers. Leans towards the feminist.

7

Self-Promotion

Are you aghast at the image the above phrase conjures up? You've just had your first story accepted and are still aglow with the glorious feeling of achievement; you're not ready to think about anything else yet . . . unless it's getting on with another story. Fine. But maybe it's time to take a break.

If you've ever attended a lecture of any kind, you will remember the glazed expressions on people's faces that appears after a while. It's a recognized fact that there's a limit to how much you can concentrate on and absorb at one time. Some teachers say 20 minutes is the maximum for adults, less for children, before a different slant is needed to keep their brains alert.

So, if you've read the previous six chapters in this book and digested them thoroughly, it's time for some light relief. This chapter is about something completely different from the workshop element of writing, and will describe to you one of the extraneous activities that make life interesting for a writer.

It's a sad fact that most of us aren't sent on nationwide publicity tours by our publishers. Nor are we constantly on TV or radio programmes. Indeed, many of us would like more promotion than we actually get (publishers, please note!). I'm not denying that promoting yourself can be time-consuming. It can also be fun and profitable, if you know the right way to go about it.

First of all, think of yourself as a business. You are now manager and head of sales for a one-man band. You have something to sell, whether it's the news of the acceptance of your first short story, your latest novel, series of articles or anthology of poems. Any business succeeds best with enough publicity to make the public aware of its existence, and who knows your particular niche better than you do?

So with that thought in mind, try to forget about false modesty because in bringing attention to your published work, you'll inevitably be bringing attention to yourself. Be prepared for this. Rid yourself of your usual reticence at pushing yourself forward (if that's the way you're made) and think of *you and your book* (or whatever) as a combined publicity package. Tell yourself repeatedly that you're now your own best publicity agent, and believe it!

Even if you get ultra-shy at the thought of promoting yourself, slide into it gradually. Get into the habit of talking about your book to family and friends whenever a suitable opportunity arises—*not* ad nauseum, but no less naturally than any of them will discuss their own jobs over the dinner table.

They will happily air their grievances over their work problems, or preen themselves when they get promotion, and expect everyone around them to be interested. So why shouldn't you sing your own praises—just a little—whether you've had a smash hit with your latest blockbuster, or had your first modest offering accepted by a provincial newspaper?

Get people used to the fact that you're a serious writer. No matter what you write, the work is important to you, and hopefully you're making money by it. Don't ever refer to your writing as just a little hobby, or something to take your mind off the kids/mortgage/weather/cost of living/state of the nation. This is your work/career, and therefore the most important thing in your life outside of personal relationships, so don't play it down. If you do, other people will quickly pick up the vibrations and they'll look on your writing as unimportant too.

Tools for self-promotion

So, if you agree with the sense in all the above, how do you go about promoting yourself without sounding like an appalling bragger and big-head? To start with, if that call should ever come asking for information about your career as a novelist, for a

63

newspaper or local radio for instance, try to have a *press kit* ready. Don't be put off—this is just a grand-sounding phrase for a few simple and basic items.

Type your own *press release*, updating it when necessary. Your press release is a third-person factual account of your career to date, your CV in fact. It shouldn't waffle or flatter. It should be written as professionally as possible, giving a crisp page of information that includes everything an interested person needs to know about you.

For instance: how long you have been writing; a brief resume of your career and successes; the names of your most recent book titles, the names of your publishers; your pen-names, if any; names of any writing organizations to which you belong; whether or not you give lectures and are available for interview; your name and address; your agent's name and address; your current publisher's name and address if you wish. At the end of this chapter is my press release, as an example of how it can be set out.

Have ready a set of *photographs* to send out when requested. You do not need to send a huge one, 3″ × 5″ is large enough for black-and-white, which is preferred, although newspapers and magazines have often reproduced my photo from an especially good, clear colour print. Head and shoulders is best, and don't send a family group and expect a busy professional person to be keen to know that you're the fourth from the left.

Photocopies of recent press cuttings are useful to send out with copies of your published book to radio or newspapers. Ask politely for the book's return when they've finished with it. Sometimes you'll get it back and sometimes not, but it's worth asking, then you can send it elsewhere—two for the price of one. Of course, you expect your publishers to do all this for you, but they don't always, and this chapter is for those of you who want to give your work that little extra push by yourself.

Business cards are a must. My cards have my photograph on them. When people come away from a meeting with a mass of little cards, the new acquaintance that they remember most will be the one with the face smiling up at them from their business card. The same idea can also be used on give-away *bookmarks* if you wish. Have them printed with your photo, your name and latest titles, and any other message you fancy.

Making contact

Make a friend of your local newspaper reporter. Most authors find that reporters frequently misquote their comments and there's nothing to stop you writing up a report for yourself and sending it to the local paper. I have written pieces in the third person, informing readers of my writing activities, sent them to a reporter, telling her to adapt or change as she wishes, and they are usually printed the way I sent them in.

She gets her usual payment. I don't get misquoted, and everyone's happy. Try to tailor anything you send to an unusual happening or event when you can because there's a limit to how many "writers' success stories" readers will take.

Inform your local radio or TV station when you have a new book coming out, instead of just waiting hopefully for your publisher's publicity department to do it. There's no harm in writing or phoning yourself. If you know somebody on a magazine or newspaper who will review your book, send it on to them or ask your publisher to put their name on the mailing list if you prefer—and if you can rely on your publisher to do so.

When you go on holiday, take a selection of your books with you or a few magazines containing your stories or articles. When you exchange personal details with holiday friends, they will invariably ask if you have any of your work with you once they know that you're a writer. (It's also proof that you really are one of those mysterious beings etc. . . .)

Give away signed copies or, if you're feeling mean, sell a few. Either way, your name will become known to the recipient and their friends, and they will probably look out for your books in the future, and pass on the news to their friends that they met a real live author! (As opposed to a dead one, presumably.)

If you write novels, then at some stage in your writing life you will probably have some foreign editions and the publishers will send you copies. What do you do with books published in French, German, Italian, Greek? There are various outlets for you to get rid of them, rather than have them cluttering up your shelves. (Keep a couple for vanity's sake, naturally.)

Some libraries have "foreign language shelves" and are appreciative at having copies donated to them. So are hospitals.

Foreign embassies may take them for distribution or, less grandly, your local council, or schools and colleages who have a summer-holiday exchange programme with foreign students. Not all students are as outgoing as one may think, and a lonely French girl may feel less homesick with a novel in her own language to read. I know this from experience.

Take the appropriate foreign edition to whatever country you are visiting. I do this and give a signed copy to the chambermaid, waitress or whoever else has been helpful, and they are always thrilled and delighted because they never realized that in Room X there was a RLA (work it out).

Large-print editions of your books may come your way. Again, several copies will be sent to you. If you don't have any poor-sighted friends or relatives who would love such a copy for Christmas or a birthday, donate these again to libraries or hospitals, or to your doctor's waiting-room.

In all cases, this is getting your name known, and will do your sense of magnanimity no end of good.

Making the most of opportunities

Always accept speaking engagements and, when you do, take some of your books with you. You may sell none of them, but the important thing is that the audience will have spent an hour or more taking in the appearance of your book-covers. Your books and your name will be familiar to them next time they go to a bookshop or library looking for something to read.

Never miss unusual opportunities. Several years ago, an American publisher brought out a book of "Romantic Recipes" contributed by romantic novelists. I was asked to send one in. I had been away for several weeks' holiday at the time, and the deadline had passed. Since I had nothing to lose, I sent the recipe anyway. It did get included in the finished book, together with details of my recently published novels, giving me a little more publicity to cookery-book fans.

I was also approached by a large chocolate firm, who were interested in an innovative promotion scheme, and wanted a

66

writer to write 12 romantic short stories. Half of each story was printed on the outside of a chocolate box, the other half inside, and my pen-name was printed on every one. It was an unusual way of being published, but profitable both in finance and publicity.

Of course you'll agree to do book-signing when asked, even for a modest first novel . . . but don't ever think of that first book as "modest". It's an achievement to finish any novel let alone get it published, and hundreds of hopeful authors envy you that precious acceptance letter and subsequent cheque, to say nothing of the marvellous day when your pristine book arrives, brand new, shiny and unopened. This is your baby, and you should be just as proud of it as if it was flesh and blood.

Interviews

If you are interviewed on TV, speak distinctly. Look your interviewer in the eye, and don't sound bored or blasé about your work or your interviewer will be bored too, and so will the viewers. Be animated without being exaggerated. Remember that you don't have to answer every question you're asked. It isn't a truth game. But don't get nasty with your interviewer, who at that moment is your Best Friend. Do as the politicians do, and learn to skirt round any awkward questions.

There are stock questions every writer is asked, particularly romantic novelists. Try to anticipate some of them, and not be taken by surprise and act coy or outraged. The tongue-in-cheek question about research for steamy novels, for instance, can be forestalled by commenting that Agatha Christie didn't have to commit murder in order to write about it!

In any interview, mention the title of your book as often and as naturally as you can without being a parrot. Remember it's your current book you're talking about and this is the one that readers will want to find in the shops tomorrow. So unless this is a general discussion about your entire career, don't harp on about out-of-print titles, no matter how fond you are of them.

Finally, never laugh at your interviewer, or try to sound

superior. And remember that, ultimately, good writing is the best publicity you can have. Promoting yourself takes time and energy, but if you enjoy being involved in your own progress as a writer, and in making your name as familiar as corn flakes, then you'll find it well worthwhile.

PRESS RELEASE

Jean Saunders

JEAN SAUNDERS began her writing career in 1965 as a short-story writer. She has published about 600 short stories, in Britain and abroad, and more than 40 novels, contemporary and historical.

As JEAN SAUNDERS she is a "Silhouette Romance" author for Simon & Schuster, USA, and published worldwide. She also wrote teenage novels under this name for William Heinemann.

Ballantine, USA (Macdonald Futura UK), published her flamboyant historical saga, *Scarlet Rebel*, with its setting the 1745 Jacobite Rebellion. A Tapestry Historical, USA (Coronet, UK), is called *Golden Destiny*, with the Indian Mutiny as its background.

As JEAN INNES she is published by Robert Hale, UK, and in the USA by several publishers. Many are published in large-print editions. A Bantam paperback was condensed as a *Good Housekeeping* choice in USA, Spain and Australia. Many of her novels are published abroad, including USA, Brazil, Greece, France, Yugoslavia, Italy, Japan and the Scandinavian countries. One book has been translated into Hebrew.

Two historical romances appeared under the name of SALLY BLAKE for Futura. But as ROWENA SUMMERS, she is now published by Sphere paperback and Severn House hardback. ROWENA SUMMERS novels are earthy and powerful. *Willow Harvest*'s background is the Somerset willow-growing and basket-making trades. *Killigrew Clay* is the first of a series of novels set in the Cornish china-clay industry. *Clay Country* is next and takes up the family saga which is continued in *Family Ties*.

In August 1986, JEAN SAUNDERS' non-fiction book, *The Craft of Writing Romance*, was published by Allison & Busby. It covers contemporary and historical fiction, which she considers an exciting project to promote the prestige of romantic writing.

JEAN SAUNDERS is a member and ex-Honorary Membership Secretary of the Romantic Novelists' Association, the West Country Writers' Association, and the Romance Writers of America. She attends and lectures at writers' groups and conferences, womens' groups, and schools. She features in publications about writers on both sides of the Atlantic, and has been interviewed on TV and radio. She is married with three children, and she writes full-time.

JEAN SAUNDERS is available for interview.

For any further information, please contact:
JEAN SAUNDERS or (Agent's name)
(addresses and telephone numbers included)

I hope you find the format of the press release helpful. You may also realize that in giving it to you, I am doing an extra bit of self-promotion. See how it works?

8

Writing a Teenage Novel

This may be something you've never even considered. Do such things exist? They most certainly do, and have been in existence longer than you may think.

Consider the following fictional problems contained in a novel: relationships with the opposite sex; poverty and war; imprisonment; adjusting to a less affluent lifestyle; the sadness of death; and family relationships. A contemporary novel, you think? It was published in 1868 by Louisa M. Alcott, and the title was *Little Women*—a novel for and about young people. There's nothing new, etc. . . .

It seems odd that, in those days, readers were quite prepared to accept the more grisly details of life and writers were ready to dwell on sorrow and despair to a degree that touched on the morbid. In more modern times, such themes became taboo for a while. Perhaps the two world wars had something with the desire to push such horrors into the background, but it's a fact that until the early 1960s, books for young people rarely dealt in any great depth with aspects of adult life other than careers and books about horses.

In the days before the 1960s, fictional parents were often conveniently disposed of in novels by a brief mention of death or, more popularly, business abroad. Sexual relationships were virtually ignored unless in terms of a passing reference to an engagement or marriage to take place at some future date.

The teenagers of today would hardly recognize those innocents of the fictional world. They themselves are more sophisticated, and so is their reading entertainment. The permissive society opened many doors, not least the need for far more realistic fiction if teenagers were to bother with reading at all.

Statistics show that teenage novels are read by young people from the age of 12 upwards. The central characters in the books are usually between 15 and 17, and the stories are for and about people like themselves.

Those who consider writing teenage novels are inclined to fall into three groups. Some think it will be easy enough, because it's a short book that can be dashed off quickly. Others shrink from the idea, feeling themselves out of touch with people who wear weird clothes, have strange hair-styles and talk in a language all their own. A third group lumps all teenage novels into the category of children's books and thinks them not worth bothering about.

They *are* worth bothering about. Teenage novels are a specialized form of writing; they are also different in style from teenage magazines, having more depth to them and not being solely confined to boy-meets-girl themes. They are written in a deceptively easy style to appeal to people whose prime interest is not curling up with a good book for company. For this one reason alone, the teenage novel needs to be sharp, entertaining and compulsive reading.

Publishers have always catered for children, but for many years all that younger teenagers were offered were books about mysteries in the Upper Sixth, secret societies in and out of the classroom, or the classics.

You may be surprised at some of the topics covered matter-of-factly in more modern books, such as drug-taking, early pregnancy and so on. Such topics may be in the minority of the subject matter used, but if handled sensitively they are acceptable themes because they cover areas to which the teenager of today can relate, whether we like it or not.

It's a valid argument that it's preferable for teenagers to read about these things in a responsible piece of fiction than in under-the-counter magazines. Such books will never commend anti-social behaviour, but the writer must also avoid any hint of moralizing or preaching or talking-down. Once that creeps in, you've lost your reader.

Know who you're writing for. That doesn't mean it's essential that you know hordes of teenagers personally but to write successfully for this market, you need to have a definite sym-

71

pathy for young people and an understanding of the problems of adolescence.

If you cringe at those way-out clothes and the sound of loud music, for instance, or keep muttering that things were better in your day and a spell of National Service would do them all good . . . perhaps you should ask yourself if these really are the people you want to write about. Your "superiority" will show through.

No, you can't like everything you see and, en masse, teenagers can be unnerving. But a writer is not writing for the gang that rampages through train corridors. You are writing for someone who wants to read a good book, and each teenager is an individual. It may help to try and picture the reader of your book before you even begin. Since most readers are girls, I shall refer to the reader as her.

Imagine her on her own, away from the influence of friends or anyone else, and she's not so very different from anyone at the same age. She will have the same basic hopes, fears and ambitions. Her outward appearance is more brash, because she has to keep up with the trends of her generation, but inside, she can still suffer agonies from the same kind of inferiority complexes that plagued you or me.

The smallest happenings are charged with drama for the teenager. Their emotions are always ready to explode, because they haven't yet learned to control them to the same extent as an adult. The spot on the chin will be a major disaster to the girl going out on her first date with a boy. If she's asked to babysit at home when she wanted to go out with friends, she'll be devastated. She'll be convinced she'll never be one of the in-crowd again. And being part of the group is all-important, being an unwilling loner the thing most dreaded. (Incidentally, the loner is always a good subject for the writer.)

Combine all this with the pressure of exams being pushed down their throats, the unemployment problem, parental pressures and anxieties, and it's hardly any wonder that rebellion is a word so often applied to teenagers.

Some years ago they were referred to as reluctant readers. It was a bad label, because it unintentionally implied that they were dull or slow-witted, and needed one-syllable words and

72

simple story-lines. That wasn't the intention at all. If teenagers are reluctant to spend their time reading, it's because they are at an age of great discovery, about themselves and about new relationships, and there are many more interesting things for them to do than sit still and read a book.

The lure of these other things is made so attractive. Who wouldn't want to watch "Top of the Pops" at 15-years old? Or spend the evening playing records with the group? Or sit in a coffee-bar all evening, or at the local disco, just talking about anything and everything? It's normal to do these things, and book-reading certainly isn't the prime interest of every teenager.

There could be other reasons for their unwillingness to read. Perhaps they live in a home where there are no books. Parents with little or a poor education can actively encourage children to ignore books, telling them they're wasting their time and should be doing something more useful.

The market

But watch teenage girls devouring every inch of the magazines geared to their interests and you'll know that the art of reading hasn't died out. There's a massive market for magazines about pop stars, records, fashion and romance.

The problem pages of teenage magazines are a real eye-opener as to how unsure of themselves the girls can be, however well they can hide it. Those are the ones that get printed in the magazines. If you ever saw some of the ones that arrive in editors' offices that could never be printed, you would be even more alarmed at the desperate cries for help from these most modern teenagers.

Boys will buy endless magazines about football, motorbikes or stereo systems. They will read books based on TV programmes like *Doctor Who* or *Grange Hill*. This should give you a strong clue as to the kind of reading that would appeal to them—fast-moving, visual plots, because these teenagers have never known a world that didn't have television in it. They're bombarded with crisp, up-to-the-minute storylines to stop the inevitable boredom taking over. If they don't like a programme, they can switch it off. If they don't like the look of a book, they won't even bother to turn the page.

If your library has a section for teenage reading, I would strongly advise anyone wanting to write these novels to take some out and read them. There have been various series in the last decade that have come and gone and so, to be as up-to-date as possible, look at the date on the copyright. In general, this is only to avoid sending your manuscript to publishers that no longer print these books, because the required content for more recently published books has not changed all that much. The teenage problems are still the same. Only the publishers have changed.

Publishers

Many publishers prefer not to publish in series, but include one or more novels aimed at the 15-plus age group in their monthly quota of new books. It pays to search out the books on library shelves to see which publishers are doing this, or write to some of them asking for their current catalogue. They are more likely to send you one if they know you are a serious writer interested in their list.

I once wrote to a selection of publishers when I did a series of talks about teenage fiction, and all were extremely helpful. In most catalogues, the little blurb beneath the titles gave a good indication of what the book was about, and the aspiring writer can glean quite a lot from the publisher's requirements in this way.

Pan Books publish a series of teenage novels called "Heartlines". These are written in the first person, which may be a hindrance to some people, since all the actions in such a novel must be experienced by the narrator and this is not as easy as it seems. But very often the writer of magazine confession-stories may find first-person teenage novels relatively easy to write, because it is a continuation of the style and viewpoint of the magazine work.

74

American publishers flood the market with anything that sells, and at the moment teenage novels are riding high. Bantam's "Sweet Dreams" is a series that is also published in Britain. So is the Simon & Schuster "Silhouette First Love" series. Both these publishers will send tip-sheets on request. Information about other teenage publishers in America can be found in various American magazines such as *The Writer* or *Romantic Times*.

Details of American markets in general can be obtained in various publications from Arthur Waite, Freelance Press Services, 5–9 Bexley Square, Salford, Manchester M3 6DB. You can also obtain the excellent *Contributor's Bulletin* from this address, which give news of new markets of every kind. To divert for a moment, I cannot recommend too highly the comfort and constant interest to be obtained from contributing to a regular writer's magazine: you will be inspired by the features from other writers and you will realize that you are not alone in your frustrations or your joys in the wonderful world of writing.

Choosing your theme

While no one can give you a blueprint for writing any successful novel, there are things to avoid and pointers to observe, that have resulted in publication instead of rejection for many beginners.

A book that was published a few years ago is John L. Foster's *Reluctant to Read*, which is in many libraries. This outlines topical themes and gives a list of publishers. The themes will still be relevant, the publishers probably not, so do your own checking as already mentioned. What is most useful in *Reluctant to Read* is the list of themes mentioned, giving you a ready run-down on which to base your novel.

Moving house, for instance, which can bring many traumas to a teenager when she has to leave all her friends and perhaps her first boyfriend, because of a family move.

Parents separated by death or divorce. A teenager can act

completely out of character when either of these things occur. A fictional story on this theme could be very moving, or written humorously or in the style of a "survival" story.

First loves or first jobs are always popular themes. Because of this, try to bring something different into your story, something unique in the writing style or content so that the editor doesn't take one look and think that here's the same tired old story again.

Conflicts with parents can cover a hundred permutations: arguments over boyfriends, too much make-up, staying out late, failing exams, keeping bad company, untidiness, or leaving home. There are also problems with new employers, teachers, other people at school, younger or older family members.

The list of possible ideas for a teenage novel is endless—but it's *how* you write the novel that will make it saleable or not.

Style

Everyone's style is individual, but certain techniques apply specifically to this kind of writing. Using fairly short sentences and paragraphs, for instance, so that the reader isn't put off by pages of dense writing that remind her of school textbooks. Don't make those short sentences too staccato or all the same length, or the tone of the book will be jerky. Intersperse short sentences with longer ones, to give a smooth rhythm to the reading. Moments of extreme tension can be conveyed by the briefest of sentences, of no more than one, two or three words.

Using crisp, up-to-date language and slang is an asset and a pitfall. If you make the novel too slangy, it will sound as if you're trying too hard, and even being slightly patronizing. Besides which, by the time the book gets into print, the current "in" words will probably be "out" and your book will have a dated feel to it, instead of being ultra-trendy as you thought.

The construction of the novel should be tight, keeping to one strong storyline rather than introducing sub-plots. Try not to use too many minor characters, particularly those who only pop in and out of the story at intervals so that the reader has to check back to see who he or she is. Those who merely enter the story for a page and then disappear probably needn't be there at all.

Test the scene in question by asking yourself if the action could happen just as well without that extra character. If the answer is yes, then cut them out. Be ruthless rather than indulgent with your characters.

Keep the actual time-span of your novel fairly short: six months or less is often the best length of time to aim for. If the span covers years, your teenager character will be an old married lady by the time the reader finishes the book. One of my books, *Nightmare* (Heinemann Pyramid), took place in about 12 hours. Another, *Anchor Man* (Heinemann), took only a little longer. If you can get a good, tight situation into a short space of time, so much the better.

Descriptive passages should be kept short and woven in between dialogue and prose; use vivid, emotive words to sustain precision of style and simplicity of storyline. There's no need to limit your vocabulary or to be over-conscious that you're writing for young people, but there is a danger of being excessively pompous and using long-winded sentences when one sharp, crisp word might do just as well.

Despite fears to the contrary, television has drawn many people back to reading, not least because of all the immensely popular "books of the series". Television gives an immediacy of action and involvement, and instant identification with characters and their problems—this is precisely what a good teenage novel should do.

There should be no delay in setting the scene, in establishing clearly the identity of the main character, and the nature of his or her problem. Ideally, the main character and the situation should appear on page one. The problem should be revealed by page two, and by the end of Chapter One, the seeds of doubt as to whether or not this problem can be resolved, should be planted firmly in the reader's mind. The reader will then be compelled to read on, to see if this character has what it takes.

You must get your reader hooked quickly. I can't stress this point strongly enough. There's no space in a teenage novel for long tedious flashbacks or dialogue between characters who have nothing to do with the story. Cliffhanger endings to chapters are the best way of ensuring that your reader won't want to put your book down. Remember that once your teenage reader loses interest in a novel, you've lost her to those other temptations of coffee bar and disco.

Nor can you afford to have a "breather" chapter: every one must move your story nearer and more logically to the conclusion, with no false trails along the way, no contrivances such as an oh-it-was-all-a-dream ending, no sense of the cavalry coming over the hill in the nick of time to put everything right.

The characters in your book should seem to be real people. In this type of book, perhaps more than in any others, reader-identification is vital. Your aim as a writer is to make your reader feel unable to put your book down; that she has to finish reading it at one sitting.

Planning a novel can take far longer than the actual writing of it. You will find that you tend to write your book over and over in your head, before as well as during the actual physical writing of it. That's good. You will be mentally discarding dialogue that doesn't fit your characters. You will be changing the construction and balance of your story. You will be honing unnecessary scenes and subconsciously perfecting your craft.

Once you get a good idea for your novel, jot it down and let it play around in your subconscious without trying to force the whole novel to emerge at once. Your subconscious is a marvellous aid to writing. It will do a lot of the work for you—if you will let it. This is a trick many experienced writers use, to let your mind become receptive and allow the bits of the plot to start falling into place like the pieces of a jigsaw puzzle.

The length of chapters in a teenage novel is a problem for some writers. Remember what I said earlier on. As a general rule, the shorter the book, the shorter the chapters. So in a teenage novel, you may have chapters of 2,000–2,500 words, or a little more. Don't feel you must stick rigidly to these limits. Be your own judge and let the chapter lengths vary a little. If you're still uncertain about stringing chapters together to produce even a short novel, think of those chapters as linking short stories, which may help to quell that sense of thinking you can never do it. You can, you know.

One of the most joyful things about being a writer is that there are no rules that can't be broken. If you are a born storyteller, almost anything else will be overlooked. But since you can't be sure of that until an editor tells you so, stick to some of the rules, at least for the moment.

Characters

Your teenage characters must be active, not passive. They go out and make things happen. They don't sit back and let circumstances swamp them. Don't skimp on characterization: know more about your characters than you put into the story, because that sureness will come through in the writing. I know my characters' hang-ups, their irritating habits, and their motivation for everything they do.

Real teenagers have explosive emotions, and so should your fictional ones. Don't be inhibited. Let them have that blazing row. Let them bang doors, burst into floods of tears, and swear if they must (avoiding four-letter words). Aim at wringing every bit of drama required out of every situation.

Let your reader assume the role of proxy heroine while reading your story. Let her know how it feels to get involved at that terrible fight at the beach; how it feels to be caught smoking in class; to realize that her mother's illness is serious, and how it feels when someone she loves dies. If your characters skim along on the surface of the story, they will have no depth to them. The stories shouldn't be all doom and gloom, but the characters must still have this essential realism.

Give your character a best friend to confide in and reveal her hopes and fears to the readers. Set her in a background your reader will understand, a comprehensive school for instance. Make her ordinary in the best sense, rather than some upper-class being who will turn readers off at once. (Unless your more well-heeled character is trying desperately to be liked, and to break some social barrier.) Give her a name like Linda or Sue, and remember one very important point: when a teenager is at the most difficult age, so is the parent. The teenage girl becomes aware of her femininity; the teenage boy realizes there are other things in life beside football, and discovers the opposite sex with a capital S.

And when does this metamorphosis take place? Often at the very time that Mum starts getting neurotic and menopausal. Dad develops a paunch and his hair starts to recede; he remembers all he intended to do with his life and time is rushing by. Here, in their midst, are these two young people with fresh new personalities, the unwitting echoes of themselves. . . .

In real life it can be hell to live through. In fictional terms it's a marvellous background for writing a book. Just a word of warning: don't be tempted to make all your teenage characters shining-faced martyrs, and their parents faded has-beens. Life ain't like that.

Listen to real teenagers talking. Study teenage magazines to find out about their interests. Watch TV programmes specially catered for them. Schools programmes are excellent for market study. Eavesdrop shamelessly, on buses, and in shops, cafés and cinemas. They're witty and articulate; sloppy and ungrammatical; knowledgeable and superior; uncertain and insular. Not so different from anyone else, really.

You thought teenage novels weren't worth writing? Shame on you. A few published ones to illustrate the range of topics are as follows:

Sky Girls by Dianne Doubtfire (MACMILLAN TOPLINERS).
Anchor Man by Jean Saunders (HEINEMANN PYRAMID)
Forgive and Forget by David S. Williams (PAN HEARTLINES).

9

How to Annoy an Editor

Dear Editor,

I'm sending my science-fiction book to you, even though I know you don't normally publish that kind of thing, and are known for your excellent cookery and gardening manuals. However, I think it would be a very good idea if you branched out, and am taking the liberty of trying you with my first book.

Yours cordially, Star Galaxy.

P.S. What do you think of the pen-name?

Dear Mr Galaxy,

Your pen-name is very original. I have never heard of another author using anything like it. As to the kind offer of your novel, if this publishing house does ever decide to branch out from our solely non-fictional outlets, we will certainly remember you.

Three guesses in what capacity.

Dear Editor,

I sent my manuscript to you last week, and I've heard nothing from you yet. I sometimes think you people aren't interested in acquiring new authors at all. I studied the *Writers' & Artists' Yearbook* meticulously and chose you as the most suitable publisher for my novel. I therefore look forward to an early reply.

Yours indignantly, Col. Edgar Smythe-Jones

The reply—and manuscript—will undoubtedly be by return of post.

Dear Editor,

I have had a most amazing life and am sure you would be devoutly interested in reading all about it. I was born the son of a Rumanian peasant and a French opera singer, and although I went to junior school on the seedier side of Paris, it didn't affect me at all, old chap. Mother had the money, you see, but she didn't want to influence me by sending me to anywhere too posh. When I was six my parents took me to Russia to study acrobatics, thinking I might have a career in the circus, but then I suffered from polio, and it was decided that my limbs would never be strong enough to support several other people while balancing a football on the end of my nose. . . . I grew rather heavy through inactivity, but still managed to develop a liking for football at 11, but alas, same problem. No strength. My father meanwhile was learning to be a builder, and since Mother and I really fancied the idea of living in a French château, Pa thought he would have a go at building one himself. Have you ever seen modern French châteaux? They're so different from the old, boring kind, with hundreds of turrets and things . . . anyway, Pa was hopeless at building and, in fact, fell off a ladder and broke his neck before he'd even got to the dining-room windows, so that was that. . . . Mother was ever so plucky and went on singing, even though her heart was breaking. You know, the show must go on and all that kind of thing . . . now, where was I? Oh yes. I'll skip the bits between 11 and 14, don't want to bore you, do I? Well, fourteen's a bit of a tricky time for a young lad, y'know, wink, wink, say no more. All the growing up bit, and learning about the body beautiful—or, by then, grossly pink and pimply in my case. I think I was turning out to be a bit of a disappointment to Mother. You sense it by all the little, unspoken things, like hiding me away in a cupboard when she had company, or pretending that the fat lump on the sofa was the dog. Anyway, old chap, to cut a long story short, I broke my leg rather badly at 14 and poor old Mumsy had to pay for me to go into a posh nursing-home because she was touring with the opera company at the time—did I tell you she was an opera singer? Oh yes, I did. . . . I say, you are following all this, aren't you? I mean, the rest of it is frightfully interesting, but perhaps I've given you enough to whet your appetite for now and you can write straight back and tell me if you'd like me to write my autobiography or not. I know you'll be dying to hear the rest of it. Incidentally, I'm 62 now, so there's a long way to cover yet. Looking forward to hearing your yea or nay.

Yours, etc., etc.

Answer—NO.

Dear Editor,

I was ever so thrilled at reading your latest romantic novel by that clever writer, Milly Bloggs. What a wonderful author she is, all those heaving bosoms and muscly thighs and things, all making your average reader palpitate over the cornflakes, to say nothing of simmering with passion between the sheets—ooh, that was ever so slightly naughty of me, wasn't it?

Anyway, what I'm getting around to is this—I've read so many of your wonderful romantic novels that I'm quite sure I could write one myself. So could you please tell me what sort of thing you'd like me to do? Just tell me if you want it set in Cornwall or Majorca and the kind of hero and heroine you want, though of course I know already that he'll be tall, dark and handsome with a matted hairy chest and ready to whip the heroine into submission if she so much as looks at him. And she'll be a thin little waif of a girl with huge blue eyes and a tip-tilted nose, and high little breasts (oops, there I go again).

I know all this because, as I said, I'm a devoted reader of your incredible novels and I could almost recite complete pages from them. So perhaps I should just go ahead and write anything that comes into my head. What do you think?

Yours with great expectations, Amanda Leigh.

Private answer, unprintable. Actual answer likely to suggest kindly that she writes her book and submits it in the usual way when it will receive the usual attention.

Dear Editor,

I am thinking of writing a novel. I have never done such a thing before, but a few things puzzle me. Do you think it would be a good idea for me to get an agent or should I send it directly to a publisher? And, if so, would you be interested in my novel? I got your name from a friend who knows somebody who writes a bit for a local newspaper, so hope you don't mind me writing to ask.

Yours hopefully, Suzanne Morris.

Dear Miss Morris,

Thank you for your letter. First write your novel, and then decide whether you want to send it to an agent or publisher. The choice is entirely yours, but perhaps I might suggest you join a writers' group for mutual help and advice.

Yours etc., etc.

Dear Editor,

I was very angry indeed to get my manuscript back from you this morning. After I sent to you for a tip-sheet on how to write romantic novels, I followed every single suggestion to the letter. You couldn't have read it properly, or you must have seen that! You said my characters should be of a certain age and appearance, and this was what I gave you—exactly. I did not set the book in the wrong location. You gave as an example the Caribbean or South America, so I used both in alternate chapters. Didn't you think it made a refreshing change to have the characters plane-hopping all the time? You said the minor characters could be a Scottish housekeeper, or a little Irish maid, or a one-legged younger brother. I included all those. You said you didn't want too many sex scenes, so I was very careful

84

to space them out, and only put one on every 25 pages—I'll send my book back to you to count, if you don't believe me. You said the dialogue should be realistic, well, I defy anyone to say that my bloody dialogue isn't realistic! Anyway, I'm so furious that you've turned my book down after all my efforts, that I doubt whether I shall ever bother to send you another one.

Yours in anger, Marilyn Frost.

Unwritten answer, thank God.

Dear Editor,

I'm sending you my article about writing an article. The idea for it came to me while I was in the bath, thinking about what to write. While I was contemplating my plastic duck, I thought, well, why not write an article about writing an article? It seemed like a very original idea to me, so I hope you'll think so too. After all, there must be thousands of people like me, thinking about nothing in particular while soaking in the bath, and you never know, you might get a lot more sent in after you publish mine. By the way, sorry about the soggy paper.

Yours, Percy Bingley.

No reply. Soggy article returned with compliments slip.

Dear Mr Editor,

I am not a moron. I know perfectly well that you are extemely busy and have no time to listen to sob stories. Which is why I would never dream of burdening you with mine. The fact that my autobiography is dramatic and heart-rending and all those other wonderful adjectives that reviewers put on bestselling books is only because my past is simply, well, dramatic and heart-rending. To be born in a hovel in Dundee and go through all the agonies of near-starvation because of a drunken mother and a layabout father is one thing but, I tell you, it's nothing to what I'm going through now. It's no fun being a single parent with six kids, living in a tenement in Glasgow. That's why I need the

85

money from writing my autobiography which I've now written and am sending to you because the books you publish seem to make a lot of money so I hope mine will too. It's not just for me, of course. It's for the six kids, poor little fatherless devils.

Yours in hope, Morag Macpherson (MISS)

Dear Miss Macpherson,

Thank you for thinking of us with your autobiography. I regret it is not suitable for our list, and wish you luck in placing it elsewhere.

Yours, etc.

Dear Editor,

What the hell are you playing at? I sent you my book two months ago and I still haven't heard back from you. I'd have thought common decency would have made you reply by now. All I've had is a snotty postcard to say you've received the manuscript. You aren't publishing it on the sly, are you, and not sending me any royalties for it? I've heard of underhand publishing tricks like that. Anyway, I'd be glad to hear from you pretty damn quick.

Yours, Willy Munroe

Manuscript returned PDQ, with compliments slip.

Dear Editor,

Thank you so much for returning my manuscript, and I do understand all your very valid reasons for turning it down. It was really very good of you to spare the time in saying so briefly and clearly why it wasn't quite suitable for your list.

Now, what I want to know is this. I'm looking at page 14, and I wondered exactly what you meant when you said that Daphne Simpson was acting out of character in several places? And why did you think Lord Winstanley was a homosexual? I would never write about such things! I'm just a teeny bit offended that you thought I would, actually, but no matter.

There's a passage in Chapter Nine that you pointed out as being obscure. Surely not? It seems quite obvious to me. Could you explain more fully what you meant? I know there are rather a lot of dead people coming into the book, but I needed to explain who they all were, and if you got a bit mixed up then perhaps you weren't quite concentrating. I know what a busy office is like, people coming in and out and disturbing the muse, and all that kind of thing. If you like, I could send the book back for you to read again. Let me know. I'll be waiting avidly for your letter or phone call.

Yours most sincerely, Hilary Powell

Unwritten reply—don't hold your breath.

Dear Editor,

My short story is really better suited for a more adult kind of magazine, but I thought I might try it on you anyway. If you think it's too sophisticated, I shall quite understand, only these days people are far more broadminded, aren't they? And a little bit of healthy titillation, to say nothing of sex, seems to go into everything you read, doesn't it? See what you think.

Yours, Chuck Rand

Answer: I'm afraid *Sea Rangers* is not ready for your kind of story yet. Try it on *Men Only*. Yours, etc.

Dear Editor,

I must say I never expected such a quick return of my manuscript. You couldn't possibly have read it in so short a time. In fact, I know you haven't. I put a hair between pages 203 and 204 and it hasn't been disturbed. I shall tell all my friends, and I'm sure none of them will be sending their books to you either.

Yours indignantly, Felicity Riley

No reply. The editor is still counting to 100 before tearing out his own hair.

Dear Editor,

I see from your tip-sheet that you are willing to read three chapters and a synopsis. This idea excites me very much, as I find the thought of writing a whole book very unnerving, and doubt if I could ever do it. But I'm sure I could manage three chapters and I suppose you mean that someone else will finish the book for me. However, the thought of a synopsis is also unnerving and I'm sure I couldn't possibly do that either. I mean, how can I know what the ending of the book is going to be when I'm still thinking about the beginning?

Anyway, I shall soon be sending you three chapters to look at, and hope you'll excuse the fact that I can't write the synopsis. By the way, I've decided to send Chapter One, Chapter Ten and Chapter Twenty, these being roughly the most exciting bits of my book that I've thought out so far. Of course, they may come in a different order if I do ever attempt to write any more of the book myself. I hope this is all right.

Yours eagerly, Josie Nelson

Dear Miss Nelson,

I am writing straight back to clarify one or two points, and to prevent you wasting your valuable time. I quite understand your difficulty in writing a synopsis, however it is preferable to have some notion of what you are going to write before you write it. Also, a synopsis gives us some idea of your capability of story construction. As to your suggestion of sending three random chapters—no, Miss Nelson, it must be the first three chapters, so that we can assess your writing ability. And no, Miss Nelson, the book must be entirely your own work.

Dear Editor,

Why did you return my novel? Is it that you have some objection to writing about the Church and politicians in general, or because you think I'm disguising—very cleverly I might add—the identities of living personalities? I have been connected with the Church myself, and am now toying with the idea of going into politics. And it would not be the first time such a person had written successful novels on those subjects. I fail to see why you were so quick in returning my novel to me, and would like some further explanation, etc., etc.

Yours, Major Allanby (Rtd)

Dear Major Allanby,

To someone of your obvious intelligence and status, I did not think it necessary to explain the finer points of libel. However, if you wish me to go into more detail, etc., etc.

Dear Editor,

Thank you for agreeing to publish my first novel. However, I wish to make some small provisos before accepting your kind offer of £350 advance. I want to do some more research on the same subject for a sequel. Could you finance me in going to Fiji to gather some new and hitherto unknown folklore material? Can you ensure that my name is in very large letters on the book jacket, and that the title of the book will have gilt lettering? There will be a paperback, of course? And I rather fancy having it in one of those bookclub editions too. I shall want to do a book-signing in several nearby towns, and also I trust that your publicity department will make every effort to get me on television and radio, since it is not worth my while to spend so many hours writing unless I can be sure of some publicity.

Yours, Anthony Villiers

Dear Mr Villiers,

I wonder if, after all, we are the right publishers for you? We are clearly too small for your grand expectations. If you prefer not to sign our contract we will quite understand and will forward your manuscript back to you forthwith.

Yours very firmly, etc., etc.

Dear Editor,

I'm sending you my short story. I know it's not very legible, but my typewriter ribbon got so faint I thought it was probably better to write the story in biro and get it sent off to you, since my friend told me how short of stories you were. She heard you speak at some writers' weekend thing. I didn't know such places existed. I bet they all have a high old time, pretending to be interested in listening to old fogies spouting. I don't mean you, of course. I wouldn't be so rude. Anyway, I saw your photo on one of your magazines once, and you looked quite young—unless it was an old photo, of course. Anyway, I hope you like my story. It's about a rabbit who turns into a human being and goes on the rampage every Saturday night. And you know what rabbits are famous for, don't you! Nudge, nudge.

Yours expectantly (whoops), Cheryl Black

Dear Miss Black,

The editor regrets . . . .

Dear Editor,

I know your magazine stories are always written in the first person, but I'm sure you'll agree that my story couldn't have been written in that way, so I hope you'll consider it anyway. The third person seemed so much better, since it's written from the viewpoint of a cat. Incidentally, I modelled Marmalade, the cat in the story, on my own little darling. I do know that your stories are all confessions (I've done my homework!) but even a cat can have problems, don't you think?

Yours in hope, Agnes James (Miss)

Dear Miss James,

Not in our magazine . . . .

Dear editor,

Iv'e been told that it dozzent reelly matter if you can spel or not, as long as you can rite a good story. Can you tell me if

that's rite? I always wannted to rite stories. Lokking for-
word to your anser.

Yours sinserley, Florrie Bexell

PS. Can you send it to my frend's adress? I don't think my
husband wood understand. He's a boxer, and very fizzical,
but dozzent think much of riters. He thinks therr all
panzzis.

This chapter is intended to give you some light relief from the
realization that there's more to being a writer than sitting down
and gazing into space and waiting for inspiration to descend . . .
but it was also meant for you to read between the lines of those
fictional letters to the editor, and to avoid any of the mistakes
that those hopefuls made.

10

Radio and Television

There are a great many outlets for the new writer on radio: from short talks to plays, "Morning Story" and so on.

Radio Talks

Radio talks, such as those used in submissions to Radio 4's "Woman's Hour", should be written as near to normal conversation as possible.

Consider your audience for a moment. The majority of it will be made up of housewives, hospital patients, car drivers, the elderly and the lonely. And there are also many people who still prefer radio to television for whatever reason.

Using normal speech patterns in your talk will produce an intimate, friendly atmosphere, as though the speaker on the radio is reaching out across the fireside to each individual listener. This is always the effect to strive for in a radio talk. Stilted language, or obscure words that few can understand have no place in short talks and will turn listeners off.

If you have some specialized knowledge of a subject which you think will be of interest to a good many people, then put it across in easy-to-follow terms. Just as in article writing, your own hobby or life style may be immensely entertaining to other people. If it interests you, it may well interest someone else.

Be prepared to read your talk yourself, if asked. For this, you will almost certainly have a voice test. Never underestimate the importance of the voice when giving your own talk—modulation, pace and resonance may make all the difference to the reception on the listeners. Deliver your talk in a good conversational style, without gabbling, and use plenty of light and shade in your voice.

Speak fairly slowly and don't keep the voice on a monotone. Smile into the microphone where possible, it doesn't matter that listeners can't see you. They will realize that a warm and friendly person is speaking to them and will respond with interest.

If women in particular are nervous, their voices tend to get higher pitched than usual, so take a few deep breaths before beginning. Sometimes the voice simply isn't suitable for radio but, if the talk is exceptionally good, a more experienced person will probably read it instead.

Unfortunately, not every writer is a good speaker, and if this is the case, you should ask yourself which is more important to you—being heard on the radio or having your talk broadcast. If it is simply nervousness that is your problem, you could record your talk on a tape at home and submit that to the producer of your choice.

To send a talk to a local radio station, try to find out the name of the talks producer from the switchboard before writing with your suggestion. It's always better to send material to someone by name if you possibly can. Tell the talks producer you've written something specially for their consideration, for a specific programme if possible, and ask if they would like to see it. Or simply send the finished talk on spec with a covering letter, in the same way as you would send a piece to a magazine.

It takes approximately two minutes to read one page of A4 in double spacing, depending on the speed of your own speech. While this will give you a rough guide as to how long your talk is, there is no substitute for reading it aloud yourself and timing it. As with written work, spoken work must be slotted into a timetable. In magazines it depends on word length. In radio, timing is of vital importance.

Many local radio stations have outlets for short talks of two to three minutes' duration, of local interest, which can be compared to short filler articles. Remember that the shorter the talk, the more you need to make every word count. Don't use up the first two paragraphs with irrelevant waffle before getting to the main points.

For instant market research, read the *Radio Times*. You will discover which programmes cater for short talks and, from then on, it's up to you to listen and do your own analysis of each programme. There is also an excellent book available called *Writing for the BBC*. This is published by the BBC, and is obtainable from booksellers or by post from BBC Publications. It can also be found on many library reference shelves.

When you are writing a talk of very short duration, such as one lasting from three to five minutes, it will only be necessary to make one important fact the pivot of your talk. Any more will clutter the main issue. For a longer talk of 15 minutes' duration, give three or four "teaching" points. In any talk, you are in effect *teaching* the listener something of which you have knowledge and, hopefully, something they wish to learn.

Rates of payment on radio vary and change, but current ones will be given in the booklet mentioned above and there will be repeat fees if the talk is used a second time.

There is a fairly limitless range of topics for radio talks, including many tiny filler slots. One-liners and brief anecdotes can be used between records or in quick-fire entertainment programmes, which also use a vast amount of joke material. Submit such material in batches to any suitable programme, preferably a named one so that the producer or performer will know that you've studied their programme and are writing with it specifically in mind.

Apart from such magazine programmes as "Woman's Hour", personal experiences can be submitted for more serious inclusion, but be careful as to just how harrowing these are. Remember the listener who may be housebound or blind, and for whom the radio is more than just something that stands on the sideboard. For many people the radio can be a lifeline, a window on the outside world, a daily companion and only friend.

Stories

"Morning Story" is a regular radio slot. Stories should be 2,150–2,250 words long and written especially for radio, which means they must be written to be heard by a mass audience and not to be read silently to oneself, as is the majority of fiction. The technique of writing radio stories is not so much different, as more intensified.

Every word must be clearly understood at once by the listener, who must be plunged straight into the story and not tempted to go and make a cup of tea because today's story obviously isn't as good as yesterday's . . . grab your listener at once by the first words you write: make them evocative, make them the best you can devise.

Consider the differences in the following two opening sentences, and think which one would make the listener instantly aware of the gist of the story.

Danny had always wanted a Rolls Royce.

Even when he was a little boy, and had looked at picture books with cars in them, it was the Rolls Royce that had interested Danny most.

There's nothing startling about the words used in that first sentence, but you don't need any more to get the picture immediately. The second sentence rambles, slowing down the thought process in the listener's mind.

From the first sentence, the listener will know at once that there's some story to come regarding Danny's wish for a Rolls Royce. Also, in those few words the query is planted in the listener's mind as to whether he ever got one. If you can get your listener curious at the outset, so much the better.

There will only be one actor reading your story, so if you introduce several characters into it make them distinctive enough for the actor to get the different nuances into his or her voice. But don't be tempted to overdo the use of dialect: for one thing the actor may not find it easy to decipher, and the listeners may be irritated by it. You may also limit your audience if a story is too localized.

Don't rule out broad Yorkshire, soft Cornish, or Cockney sparrow, all of which can enrich a story . . . but go easy on those exaggerated idioms of speech. In other words, don't make caricatures of your characters.

Sometimes a published story can be adapted for radio. You've probably heard that phrase often enough. If you have a published short story that you think will transpose, the fact that it's been published in a magazine or newspaper doesn't stop you offering it to radio, remembering that you may need to change the length and modify certain words and phrases.

You may even have a few unpublished stories languishing in a drawer that might just be more suitable for radio than the magazines they were originally written for. Think of your audience when you consider your theme and characters and see if any of those forgotten stories can be re-hashed in a different style. Nothing should ever be wasted. The germ of an old story can often spark you off for writing something new. If it inspired you once, it can do so again.

Plays

The radio play can be of varying lengths. Check with issues of the *Radio Times* to see the current requirements. The fact that you once knew there was a "Wednesday Afternon Play" or whatever, does not necessarily mean there is one now, so don't waste your time guessing. Be professional in your market research, which to me makes the process of being a writer all the more interesting.

A writer's life is never dull. If you find it so, perhaps you should be thinking of doing something else!

Radio plays will reach a specific audience, depending on the time of day that they are broadcast. Keep this in mind when choosing your background, characters and plot. A suitable play for mid-afternoon may not necessarily be right for a more sophisticated late-night audience. Conversely, a more risqué theme may be better suited to late-night listening.

As with all writing, the general guide of the shorter the play, the fewer the characters, equally applies to radio. In fact, your play may have more chance of acceptance with fewer characters—providing you have a strong and dramatic enough story to tell. Remember this is radio *drama*.

When it is broadcast, the first thing listeners will be aware of is the momentary silence after the opening title and the name of the author. From then on, the play must stand on its own.

Your listeners are drawn into your makebelieve world by the first words you give your characters to say, so make them as significant as you can. Radio drama is all dialogue. The listener cannot turn back the page to see what was said earlier. If you have made your characters too much alike, the listener will have difficulty in separating them in his or her own mind. Each of your characters must be as individual as possible. Their voices, temperaments, personalities, ages and lifestyles must come alive for the listener, who may be intending to do half a dozen other things when the play begins. Your aim is to make your dialogue so riveting that the listener simply has to stop all those other jobs, and listen to your play.

You may now be thinking that "character is all" in a radio play. But characters without motivation are like ships without rudders, tossing aimlessly about and never getting anywhere. Give your characters actions to perform, logical reasons for their reactions to one another, and sufficient conflict in the plot, and you have the basis for drama. The play that meanders along with no structure will leave listeners dissatisfied. The play that fizzles out with no conclusive ending will infuriate them.

Even if you have trouble with fictional dialogue, don't rule out the possibility of writing radio drama. You can't really know which branch of writing will suit you until you try it and, despite any dialogue difficulties you may have in writing short stories for instance, it may just be that the prose style of fiction has inhibited you. Drama may be your unsuspected forte after all.

In any case, always read your dialogue aloud. You will certainly need to do so when writing a play, to get the timing right. If a play calls for 30 minutes, don't produce a script of 24 or 41 minutes and think that the Drama Department will cut it for you. You will be thought an amateur for not getting it right in the first place, and a careless writer for not troubling to find out.

Reading your own play aloud will also alert you to the difficulties of pronouncing certain words that you may want to change. It's diffcult to say "sixth sense", for instance. An actor may well prefer to avoid such phrases, so the author who can think of a good substitute for any tongue-twisters will earn the actor's approval at least.

You will also get the feel of the drama yourself if you record the whole thing onto tape and play it back several times. Leave it for a while before you play it for the first time, and all the little flaws you overlooked will become more apparent. At this time, try to ignore the inflexions of your own voice—as long as they don't distract from the overall shape and movement of the play, which is what you should be concentrating on at this stage.

Try to be as objective as you can about your play. Always try to think of it as being written by someone else, and therefore be as critical about it as if you were just hearing it on the radio for the first time. While you listen, ask yourself the following list of questions.

- Am I immediately involved in the characters and their problems and/or situations?

- Do I like these characters and am I intrigued or amused by the predicament in which the author has put them?

- Is the central theme of the drama strong enough to sustain my listening capacity when the sun is shining and the beach is nearby, and I'd much rather be outside in the fresh air?

- Is the play continuing to hold my interest at the halfway point, so that I'm still not aware of any predictable ending?

- Is it easy for me to forget that they are fictional characters and to think of them as real people?

- If these characters were real, would I like them?

- Am I finding the sentences too long and involved, so that the dialogue is turning out like speeches, and is it sometimes hard to follow who is talking?

- Is my attention easily distracted from the play?

You may find it an interesting exercise to think up more questions for yourself, and if the answer to any of them is the wrong one, you will know where to tighten up your writing. But don't get so carried away by your own analysis that you take all the life out of your play in the process and pare it down to nothing. The end result may be self-destruction.

Writing for television

Writing for television is something that many people dream about. The financial rewards are high. Your name on the credits of your first TV play that millions will see, is enough to make any writer swell up with pride for a good two seconds. That's about how long your name will be on the screen. It will also be printed in the *Radio Times* or the *TV Times*, and may be splashed on the entertainments page of your local newspaper. (Probably with a rundown on how you wrote it in snatched half-hours between taking the kids to school or commuting to the office and doing a "proper job".)

I am not attacking the prestige of being a writer for television, merely stating plainly that in terms of public exposure, the TV writer's work has nothing like the impact of a single novel. But for glamour and glitz, it is undoubtedly a heady thing to be known as a TV writer.

Plays

Most people will think first about writing the TV one-off play. Probably the half-hour or one-hour, depending on what is currently being used. Since most people are considering this idea—including the professionals, the well-known playwrights, the regulars, and the sought after personalities courted by the TV companies—what chance do you have of getting your play read? (This is assuming that you've finally written it, that it conforms to length and timing, and has been set out in the appoved format.)

A book obtainable from libraries explaining the intricacies of television, including details of layout of scripts and so on, is called *Writing for Television in the Seventies* by Malcolm Hulke (A. & C. Black). Don't let the word "Seventies" put you off. The late Malcolm Hulke had a canny eye for what was needed to make a script appeal to a producer, and all legible scripts will be read. Write to the Script Department at the BBC or commercial TV stations, for sample scripts to study, if available.

This also applies to radio: write to the programme of your choice and request sample scripts.

So what makes a good TV play? Your own preferences will tell you the sort that you enjoy and, although you are writing a play to appeal to a mass audience, the old rule still applies. If you're not interested in your own subject, the essential spark in the writing won't come across. So, first of all, be enthusiastic about your own storyline and characters.

Don't put a cast of thousands into your TV play. Simple economics will tell you the reasons for this. Similarly, don't set your play in a variety of exotic locations or grandiose settings. A writer such as Colin Welland may persuade the producer to take his cast to Australia to record half a dozen scenes in the Outback. As a new TV writer, it is highly doubtful that your play would receive the same reception.

A play using only a few sets and characters clearly has an advantage—providing your play has enough drama in it to carry this through. Avoid too many "flashback film sequences" and try to get a sense of immediacy into your play. Scene changes should be smooth, without the characters seeming to dodge about like jack-in-the-boxes.

The contemporary play has more chance of being accepted than a historical one. Use up-to-date problems and dramas to which the majority of viewers can relate, either from your own experience or from media coverage.

Comedy

Comedy scripts are a gamble, but what isn't in the writing business? If you are a naturally funny person, with a quick wit and a mind that sees the humorous angle in ordinary situations, you may find situation comedy comes easily to you. You may decide to write an episode on spec, with brief outlines of future episodes, and send it to the company of your choice.

You may prefer to send just an idea to the Script Department and ask if there would be any interest in it. If your intention is to write the episodes yourself, it would still be preferable to submit one as above to demonstrate your writing skills and to show exactly what you have in mind. Alternatively, you could simply sell the idea and agree to having your name on the credit list, while more experienced writers produce the scripts, and you receive a royalty payment each time the programme is put out. But be warned. It would have to be a *very* good idea.

Don't send in scripts for comedy programmes that are already being shown. They will probably have been recorded months ago and the series will be complete before it ever appears on the screen.

There are many instances in which you see a whole list of contributing writers credited for a comedy programme. As in radio, you can send in batches of small sketches, or even one-liners. Be topical with such gags. Be clever without being obscure. Audiences will want to share the joke, not sit in their living-rooms with blank faces, being tempted to switch off. Such a reaction will not endear the writer to the TV company either.

Magazine programmes

If comedy is not for you, it might be worth writing something for a magazine programme. If you can, submit it on tape as well as in script form. The programme editor will hear your voice, and may be more inclinded to ask you in to the studio for a voice and vision test. If you are very keen, and have access to a video camera, you could even get yourself filmed doing your own little piece, and send that in.

Every region has its own magazine programme of local interest, and more serious topics for general discussion. In effect, this is the article in vision. Have something to say, and know how to say it. That is really the secret of all successful writing, for whatever medium.

11

Talking about Writing

Since the last chapter dealt with the spoken word as much as the written one, this seems a good point to stop and consider something that will invariably crop up sooner or later in your writing career. That is the request to speak to a group of strangers about your writing.

Do you draw back immediately and say you could never do such a thing? Perhaps you never thought you could write for publication, either. Now, you're starting to realize that it may not be such an impossibility after all.

I'm not pretending that talking about your work in public for the first time can be anything but nerve-racking. But whether you're being asked to speak at your first or your fiftieth engagement, try to keep one thing uppermost in your mind. *You* have something that this audience want to hear, and they've especially chosen *you* to tell it to them.

This was the thought I kept uppermost in my mind when I was asked to speak to Bristol Writers' Circle about 15 years ago. Nervous? I was terrified. My knees quaked so much I had to lean against the table to support myself. But, when the moment actually comes and you look at that sea of faces in front of you, you have to realize one essential thing. If you don't open your mouth and start speaking, nobody else is going to! And unless you want to look a complete idiot, you'd better sound as though you know what you're talking about! But you do, don't you? Otherwise, they wouldn't have asked you, a published author, to come and talk to them about your work. So it's back to square one.

You may eventually be asked to speak to a wide variety of people. Each group should be approached differently so don't think you can give the same talk every time. Always judge your audience, do your homework about them beforehand, and thoroughly prepare your talk. If I am asked by phone or letter to speak on a proposed date, I try to ascertain the number of people who are likely to be there. If it's a group of writers, I find out their general interests and if they are mainly beginners or more experienced, and so on.

Sometimes you will talk apparently "off the top of your head", without referring to notes, I have found this informal method popular with non-writers such as women's groups, churchwomen's guilds and so on. There is a more chatty atmosphere in a group such as this, and you play it accordingly.

Whoever your audience, whether they've paid to hear you or if you're doing it for love, aim to make your listeners warm to you. Be professional, authoritative, but never adopt a starchy, cleverer-than-thou attitude. If you have some amusing anecdote to tell against yourself, why not? You're not God, are you?

Talking to children

I recently spoke to several classes of junior-school children. I racked my brains to think what they would most want to know. As it happened, they were intensely interested in everything that made an author "tick". The questions after the talk ranged from whether I ever used vampires as "heroes" to using specific names of boys and girls in the class. Afterwards, they wanted my autograph, some on extra bits of paper—I suspect to sell to other classes—some of them on the backs of their hands, probably to their parents' fury.

To interest nine- and ten-year-olds meant giving a short, lively talk that gave them the confidence to realize that eventually they too could write for publication, if they wanted to. I took along my first offerings into print to show them.

Remember that *visual props are always useful*. I showed them the crossword puzzles and riddle-me-rees I'd written years ago for *The Brownie* magazine (see Chapter One) and they went through the word puzzles with me, cheering when they solved them. Inhibited by an author? Not on your life.

Was it a waste of time talking to schoolchildren? Don't ever think so! The rewards can be far-reaching, apart from the pleasure in having such an attentive audience. Children grow up and become adult readers. Children tell their mothers about the author who came to school and talked to them. Mothers take out library books written by that author, perhaps simply out of curiosity, and hopefully you have gained another reader.

The hardest children to reach are the fifteen-year-olds who would far rather be doing something else than listen to a visiting author (see Chapter Eight). You can't afford to let their attention wander for a moment. Talk to them about the things they understand; about pop or football magazines whose editors pay for letters and anecdotes, etc. Mention the ability to make money and they'll be hooked.

As always, tailor your talk to the needs of the age group. When I talk to schools, I always donate one of my teenage books to the school library; signed, of course. Asking the children what they would like written in it is a way of having your ears deafened, but also draws them into your circle, and makes them feel that this book is especially for them.

I use a different technique in talking to groups in schools than that used for women's groups. I use reference cards with brief notes on them. A class of unblinking, sophisticated teenagers can unnerve a speaker faster than any other group, so it pays to have a new topic ready at a glance while you catch your breath.

Preparation

For other talks, I write a fairly comprehensive speech. At a writers' conference, where the audience will understand immediately when I mention writers' blocks and the pros and cons of having an agent, I read my speech many times beforehand, referring to it during the lecture, while looking at my audience as much as possible.

Personal eye-to-eye contact is important. When giving out a piece of information, each peson likes to think you're helping him or her alone. Information is what an audience wants, particularly an audience of writers, so always give them time to scribble down some of the points they think particularly relevant to their needs. It's rewarding to a speaker to see people jotting down notes. You know for certain then that you've given them something they want to hear.

Of course they're intensely interested in how you wrote that bestseller, or sold that set of articles to a camping magazine, or broke into the poetry market or whatever. But what they really want to know is how *they* can do it. So always *give them some information*. I've listened carefully to people's reactions after they've heard a talk and it's surprising how many will say they didn't get much out of a speaker, simply because they didn't get anything to write down and peruse later.

The conclusion to draw is that listeners simply feel they're not getting value for money if they can't take notes. The more experienced writers in your audience will just listen and absorb, but beginners will take copious notes and will really feel that they've been helped.

Pay attention to the *way* you talk. It's a mistake to try and plum up your regional accent for the occasion. Your accent is part of *you* and therefore an extension of your own personality. It's far more important to speak distinctly and slowly enough for people to take those notes. Don't babble. Listen to yourself on a tape-recorder to test the inflexion of your voice, and (be honest) to find out how boring you may sound and why.

We never hear our own voices except in our heads. Other people know what we sound like better than we do, unless we record ourselves or, better still, see ourselves on video, talking and gesticulating, and making full use of all those little mannerisms we didn't realize we had!

Don't let your voice fall away at the end of sentences, so that the listener misses the punch words. Never be afraid of pausing for your listeners to digest what you're saying. Most speakers new at the game surge on from sentence to sentence, and are afraid of silences. The result is like listening to an express train rushing through a busy station—gone before you can see where it's going.

Give your listeners time to write down any addresses you give them and don't rush on to the next so that they are made dizzy by a flood of information.

Beware of making obscure jokes and never start your talk with a joke which may fall flat and unnerve you. One rule I strictly adhere to is never to start a talk with an apology. Your listeners won't feel sorry that you didn't have time to prepare your talk/you've just moved house and lost your notes/the dog had to be put down/this is the third talk you've given this week, so you're feeling pretty tired, and they're lucky to see you here at all. . . . They'll just be irritated that this isn't the speaker they've come to hear and probably paid good money for the privilege.

Remember that while you're standing head and shoulders above them in your published state, you're their undoubted tinsel god for a brief while, so let them enjoy it the way you enjoy hearing other speakers.

However amusing your anecdotes, be professional in the way you deliver them. That means paying as much attention to the first sentences of your talk as in those of your novel or article.

Speaking on radio and television

You may be asked to speak on radio or television. As opposed to submitting a talk or play or story, this is *you* talking about yourself and your first book/your career to date/your biography of Queen Victoria. . . . On radio, you're invisible, but once you see yourself on television, believe me, all those little mannerisms you don't realize you have will make you cringe.

Sit as straight and still as you can, and if waving your hands about is a part of *you* (as it is of me), curb it a little. Don't curb it completely though, or you will end up smothering your own identity in your wish to be serene and composed, and will look robotic instead.

If you are speaking into a microphone for the first time, it may be something of a shock to hear your own voice magnified. My first experience with a microphone was at a prestigious gathering of writers in London, where I had adjudicated a competition for the Society of Women Writers and Journalists. The president of the Society at that time was the late Joyce Grenfell. She gave me an invaluable tip for speaking into the mike: Always remember to sound your d's and your t's, and the rest will take care of itself. Try it. It works.

Speaking after dinner

As an after-dinner speaker, keep those anecdotes short and snappy; don't be tempted to try, in 15 minutes, to teach your sleepy and well wined-and-dined listeners how to write books. That's not what they want. They may be pleasantly dozing, but you must be as sparkling as the wine and only as informative as an easily-digested frothy dessert.

Finally, a few words to describe what I consider the ideal speaker. Approachable, always, Human, of course. Never so self-important that you forget how it felt to be struggling, unpublished, and in the doldrums after endless rejection slips when everyone else you knew seemed to be on the way up.

Never laugh at the most basic questions you are asked. A speaker should never be unkind. It takes courage to ask what everyone else seems to know. You may be asked a question to which you've already given the answer in your speech. The rest of the audience may groan. As the speaker, you should not.

That person spoke up and asked what they unfortunately missed, perhaps because they were busily writing down some other gem of your speech. So address yourself to them alone, be sincere and helpful. Answer honestly, then glance around. You can bet that more of the audience than your questioner will be scribbling down your words.

Despite all the statistics produced by learned people, we all have different absorption levels when it comes to taking in facts, and different levels of concentration too—always allow for that. Never make your speeches too long. Also, one last invaluable tip: when first approached to speak, always ask the secretary to give you a time limit. Write your speech and then read it aloud, timing yourself by the clock. This is the method I use, and it works.

Since the first talk to Bristol Writers' Circle, I've given dozens of talks. The reaction has varied. Not all of them have been brilliant talks, nor were all received with spectacular success. But the nervousness grows less, the sure touch develops, and the proudest moment in my writing/speaking career came when I was asked to be a main speaker at the Writers' Summer School in 1986 (more details of this later.) I had been attending the annual school then for 14 years and, for me, the night of my talk was an undoubted highspot in 20 years of writing. In front of 350 people, I gave it everything I had. My reward was a standing ovation. I shall never forget it.

12

First Novel, First Page

In my book *The Craft of Writing Romance* (Allison & Busby), I describe the first page of a romantic novel as being the window to a wonderful Aladdin's cave within. Unless the window is bright and attractive enough to lure the customer inside, she'll never know what delights she may be missing.

This quote is true of any novel. Unless your reader is intrigued by that first page, he or she will probably not bother to look at any of the next 200 or more—however well-written they may be.

A published novel on the shelf of a bookshop has all the trappings to lure the reader inside: the exciting jacket, with a tempting illustration depicting scenes from your book; and the title, which you have chosen yourself, to further tell the reader what the story is all about. Added to all that, there will be a blurb on the back of the book, and another inside the jacket, which tell the reader in advance that here is a Western, a historical romance, or whatever. The reader is already well aware of the mood and genre of your book before even opening it.

When you send your novel to an editor, all that will be seen is a pile of manuscript pages, typed as neatly and professionally as possible, without the advantage of all those other alluring props.

This one fact alone should make you see how essential it is to get that first page right. Spend as much time as you need to on it. If you're not completely happy with it at first, come back to it when you're well into the book, or even when the book is finished, to make those final small adjustments or that drastic revision. Whatever it takes, the first page of a novel is the one that needs more care than any other.

A full-length novel can be anything from 50,000 words in length to a blockbuster of 250,000, according to the needs of the book itself, and also to the demands of the publisher.

It can also be of many different types: the so-called straight novel; the romantic novel; the Western; science fiction; the crime novel; the thriller; the espionage novel; the historical saga; the occult novel; the glitzy novel; the children's novel; and the fantasy novel. There are other genres and within them all come a range of variations on each theme.

So, the first thing an author has to decide is which particular type of novel he or she is going to write. This may well have been decided long ago, by the author's nature, temperament and inclinations. The history buff may well have a serious historical novel buried inside, just aching to be written. The out-and-out romantic may be longing to write another *Gone With the Wind*.

The prime role of the author in fiction is to be an entertainer. In order to achieve this, the author must become deeply involved. If the novel is to be a romance, then the author must be capable of understanding the emotions of each of the central characters. A historical novel must contain more than the general atmosphere of the time in which it is set: it must be filled with the tiniest details that make every sentence in the book convey the flavour of the chosen period, making the story and characters totally authentic. So, a little about research, which cannot be ignored.

Research

Research comes into every kind of writing, so don't be frightened off by the word. If you don't know a fact concerning police procedure, you look it up or ask someone. If you're setting your book in some exotic country, at the very least you take the trouble to check its position on the atlas! For the historical novelist, there are many areas of research to consider.

One of the easiest traps for the beginning historical novelist to fall into is getting the language wrong. Not by the obvious mistakes of letting an Edwardian heroine wear Victorian clothes, but by the very words an author uses that can grate on a reader if they're out of context. I recently read a novel that was set in England in 1066. In this book an English noblewoman referred to her baby as having "gas" instead of "colic", which jarred on me immediately.

Other pitfalls can easily be overlooked. You can't really allow an electric glance between hero and heroine before electricity was invented, for instance. Some words may be historical, yet sound oddly modern and are best avoided. If they sound doubtful to you, change them.

Other clangers. . . . You can't have telephone calls before 1876, or have letters arriving from overseas faster than a sailing-ship could deliver them. You can't hitch up your heroine's skirt with a safety-pin before 1849, or give your hero a wristwatch while a pocketwatch was the only timepiece to be seen adorning gentlemen.

In one of my books, *Scarlet Rebel*, set at the time of the Jacobite Rebellion, I dearly wanted my hero and heroine to be married romantically over the anvil at Gretna Green. It seemed a simple enough scene, except that during my research I discovered that such marriages weren't sanctioned until the early 1800s—and this of course, was 1745. Any Scottish innkeeper could perform the ceremony, and I had to settle for that, although it was never quite the same as Gretna Green. . . .

A children's author must have the capacity to enter the mind of a child and see things from a child's delightfully innocent perspective. No phrases in the writing that a child would never use, for instance. No knowledgeable bits of information that would be beyond the scope of the child reading the book or, more importantly, the child character in it.

A crime novelist must understand the workings of the police force and also the criminal mind, and must therefore be something of a psychologist. Research for crime novels must be one of the most exacting tasks, yet there is such a mass of material available to help. Books of every description can be obtained for research purposes, ranging from methods of poisoning victims to effects and detection rates of poisons used, to give one example alone.

In every case, one research book will lead to at least half a dozen others by looking at the bibliography in the back of the book. The books listed there will have been used as source material by the author, or are included as suggested further reading.

Other kinds of novels will spark off their own sources of research material, including the relevant publications on any subject, such as occult or science-fiction magazines.

My own research on any subject, for contemporary romantic and for historical novels, begins in the children's library. For clarity of explanations, you can't beat it, and more detailed research can come later.

Getting started: finding ideas

So, having got the matter of research out of the way, how do you actually begin? For most published novelists, it all starts with an idea, a thought, perhaps a line of overheard conversation or some magnificent background that simply has to be written about. In othe words, beginnings are as diverse as authors, and there is no one statement to describe adequately how any author finds the words to begin.

What is common to most is that they have an overall wish to sit down and write the novel. Many successful authors will tell you that much of the novel is "written inside the head" before any words are put down on paper. I concur totally. The idea is the seed that floats around in my subconscious, growing little by little until it sprouts roots and tendrils and begins to assume a shape.

Capturing an idea can be as elusive as catching a breeze. It may seem spectacular when you first think of it; then you realize it has no substance. It was only an idea after all, which is why it has to be worked at, to develop into the fully fledged and beautiful entity that you hope your novel is going to be.

Get your idea down on paper as soon as possible. You now have something concrete to look at, to think and dream about, to enlarge upon. An idea that once came to me was from one of those overheard pieces of disembodied dialogue that we all experience. A mother was sending her child to the shop for a loaf of bread, and telling her not to come back if she lost the money . . . the sort of unfortunate remark that all harrassed parents can be guilty of making in moments of stress. A non-writer would probably think no more about it—except to feel noble, perhaps, that she wasn't the nagging mother concerned. But it started me thinking. Supposing the child took the mother's words seriously? Supposing she did lose the money and was afraid to go back home? Supposing I changed these characters a little, and considered it for the basis of a novel?

The end result of all this speculation was a teenage novel, *Roses All the Way* (William Heinemann). My main character was a teenage girl, annoyed at having to stay in and look after her seven-year-old brother. She is sent to the shop with a little red purse to buy some bread. . . .

The original overheard dialogue alone wasn't enough to inspire a novel. The initial idea rarely is. But once that good old receptive inquiring mind of the author gets to work, asking questions of any situation, the results can surprise you.

Another idea came from my wish to write a novel set around the Indian Mutiny. Just that. I had no characters in mind. I knew nothing more about it, so obviously had to rely heavily on research before I could even begin. What transpired was to consider the kind of people involved at that time.

Many Scottish regiments were then stationed in India, giving me a clue as to the character of my hero, until then undecided. Prominent also, was the East India Company and the dwindling band of exotic Indian princes and their little empires. Another clue. My heroine could be the daughter of an East India Company man attached to one of these principalities, thus bringing in all the colour of regal India as a wonderful comparison with the holocaust of the Mutiny.

This was how I built up the background of *Golden Destiny*, a Tapestry historical romance, published in America. A bonus was that I realized I could use the previous story of *Scarlet Rebel* as a legend, handed down through the Scottish hero in *Golden Destiny*, thus forming a link between the two books. American romance readers, in particular, are very fond of this kind of continuity in character and plot.

The above two ideas, although depending on outside influences to decide on my characters, should still be pointing you towards one truism: novels are about people. However glamor-

ous or seedy the background, it is the characters who must live
and breathe throughout the story.

Openings

There are various ways to begin a novel: start with some basic
problem concerning your characters; start at a time of decision
for the main character; start with a good strong scene; start with
a splendid setting, bringing characters quickly into play. Any of
these, or a combination of two or more can be used to begin a
novel. It all depends on the author.

The following passages are six openings for various types of
novels. There are no titles given, no cover illustrations, no
external props. Each opening is constructed to bring the reader
instantly into the setting, with characterization defined or hinted
at right from the beginning. No explanation of genre is needed.
Read any one of these openings, and you should know instantly
what the following pages were to be about.

1. Harry Bailey shrugged into his black raincoat and belted it
    tightly. Either it was shrinking or he was putting on a few
    pounds. He reminded himself to call in at the police gym for
    a work-out sometime soon.

    It was an incongruous thought, Harry realized with
    distaste, when he was on his way to investigate a murder.
    The poor sod whose body had been washed up on the beach
    that morning wouldn't be worrying about keeping in shape
    ever again.

    Nor should Harry right now. CID work was supposed to
    rule out such basic human feelings, wasn't it? It was part of
    the price you paid. There were times when Harry thought
    grimly that it all but emasculated him.

2. The elegant ship glided majestically through the mirrored
    waters of the Indian Ocean, her sails desperate for the
    merest breath of wind. Lady Arabella Forbes, youngest
    and loveliest daughter of the Duke of Havers, regretted

once again the obligatory heavy skirts and petticoats she wore. Her fingers were taut around the delicate pearl and ivory of her fan, trying to agitate the air as she watched for the first hint of land, excitement smothering the intense discomfort of the voyage.

"Please come away from the rail, my lady," pleaded her old nurse. "This heat will be ruinous for your complexion."

"Don't fuss, Nancy dear! It's even hotter in that appalling cupboard they call a cabin. You go below if you must, but I shall remain. Captain Peters will be strolling the deck soon, and I would speak with him—"

"Unchaperoned?" The woman said, scandalized.

3. A thousand stars exploded in dazzling homage around Freta. Illuminated in their light were the silver-clad forms of the Gava people, gliding now into their delegated positions at first moonglow to observe the ritual throning.

Freta, queen of the seventh universe, waited to receive the unknowns of this newest galaxy, her mask-like beauty disguising the clutch of fear she felt beneath the gilded robes of majesty.

She was surrounded by sky-stalwarts and loyal mutants, by all the higher and lesser subjects from near and distant stars and moons, but who knew whether these Gavas, with their scaly reed-like bodies, were destined to be friends or foes?

4. Hank Sibley hoisted his gun-belt a fraction higher, his fingers caressing the ivory grip of his Smith & Wesson. The cold touch of the metal gave him comfort and a sense of security he needed badly. Below the ridge where he crouched, waiting for Keller, sunlight shimmered and danced on the long dusty trail.

The minutes passed, merging into hours, and the slow trickle of sweat curled around Sibley's neck, running down between his shoulderblades and adding to his desperation. He had been hunting Keller for three months and it was long past time for a showdown, but lately he had begun to get the gnawing feeling in his gut that it was Keller who had become the hunter, and he the hunted.

5. Amanda hesitated for just a moment longer, although there was really no turning back now. Through the Agency, she had signed the agreement that now made her Personal Assistant to the dynamic Greg Power, multi-millionaire and land-developer.

Power by name and power-mad by nature, Amanda thought with uncharacteristic cynicism, still wondering just what kind of man was too busy to interview a prospective employee himself, and who needed a signed agreement to ensure that she would stay for at least six months!

Amanda caught sight of her reflection in the dark mirrored glass of the plush office building. Petite, with a cloud of red-gold hair around her shoulders and delicate features, she looked outwardly vulnerable, but was well able to take care of herself, she thought with a surge of defiance.

She would need to, if Greg Power's reputation with attractive young women was to be believed. She pushed open the swing doors of the Power building. There was no point in speculating. She was soon going to find out for herself.

6. The great and wonderful idea came to Simon in the summer holidays. It hadn't rained for days, and his face was rosy with excitement as he sat back on his heels beneath the hay-rick. It didn't matter that grass and straw tickled his bare knees. There were more urgent things to think about.

"I can borrow my brother's tent," he said to the others. "He never uses it now. What can you get, Porky? We'll need a torch and blankets, and biscuits, and bottles of lemonade—"

Simon waited eagerly to see what the other three would think. He was the oldest and they looked to him as their leader. He saw Porky fidget, but the eight-year-old twins spoke together as usual.

"We can get biscuits," Janie said. "Our Mum always has biscuits in the tin—"

116

"And cakes," Gavin said importantly.

Porky sniggered. "You two are like parrots. We'll need more than biscuits and cakes for a weekend in the woods!"

Simon looked at him more hopefully. For a minute he'd thought Porky was going to pooh-pooh his idea.

"You're not too scared then, Porky?" he said craftily.

"Don't be daft. I'm not scared of anything!"

In all those openings, you got some idea of the central character of the novel, the one around whom the story is going to revolve. In all of them, you saw the setting, you felt the atmosphere, you got a sense of drama, of conflict, of a novel that is going to progress because of the seeds the author has sown so early on. In other words, all of those openings would entice a reader into the book, because he or she would be wondering what was going to happen next.

You won't find any of these examples in published novels. I don't know, any more than you do, what is going to happen next. I constructed them all to illustrate the techniques of getting the reader's interest right at the beginning.

Despite the fact that I have never written a children's book, a science fiction, a Western or a whodunnit, I slipped into the role of the characters and their backgrounds.

If you wonder how I knew that a Smith & Wesson pistol had an ivory grip, I looked it up—I am simply an author with an imagination and a wish to get the details right. So are you, presumably, or you wouldn't have read this far. If not, then I hope that at least you are beginning to understand the way in which a writer's mind works.

What has happened now, of course, is that I feel tempted to go on with every one of the stories I began as mere examples! They have intrigued me. So, if you feel you could never write a novel, perhaps you could just try writing an opening for a start, bringing into play all the things I've mentioned. You too, may be so intrigued by your own beginning, that the follow-up for the story will begin to take shape in your mind.

The follow-up

After the crisp, emotive beginning, where do you go next? In the above examples, I don't know. They were little more than ideas. In creating characters and settings to suit a particular genre, I hadn't thought farther ahead. I certainly could, if I chose. There is enough there to get me going. This is just one of the infinite number of ways of starting a novel, to get those creative juices flowing and to put your characters into whatever situation you devise.

Other writers will say they couldn't possibly begin like this. That they must do detailed character studies first of all, getting to know their characters inside out before they even begin to write. That's fine, if that's the way they work. What I'm trying to do here is suggest an alternative way for the beginner who finds that a little daunting, and the thought of developing a plot in which to fit those characters even more difficult.

After all, when you've written a detailed character study of a person, what have you got? Nothing more than a detailed character study of a person.

If you construct an intriguing opening scene like the ones I've written, you have a cameo picture of your character, you have some movement in the story, some hint of where it will be going. You have something to work on. Now is the time to ask yourself the kind of questions given in all the previous exercises in this book. Now you can build on what you already have and suddenly it doesn't seem quite such an impossibility to create something out of nothing.

In the first example of the above openings, you would ask yourself why Harry Bailey seemed so disillusioned with his life. Was there a background there that was going to affect his future? Was the dead man washed up on the beach going to have any personal meaning to him? (Think of the different plots presented if the man was his son, his brother, his wife's lover. . . .) Is he really going to seed, and would the introduction of some female character change all that? Could he become involved in some police scandal, innocently or through his own guilt? Is he going to stay with the police or change direction completely? Where is this book set? There is the mention of a beach. Scarborough, perhaps? Cornwall? Barbados?

By now, everyone reading this could be building up an entirely unique picture of Harry Bailey and his circumstances, and so far I haven't even mentioned his appearance, except that he's putting on a bit of weight. You have yet to supply his looks, mannerisms, age, habits and so on.

It can be a difficult thing to conjure all this up out of thin air, but by producing the first scene in a novel, then pausing while you work through the character study and all the possibilities for the plot, it can ease the new writer into making that elusive start, which so many put off because they simply don't know where to begin.

I hope you'll consider this method as an alternative to slaving away trying to find everything at once. Life rarely works like that. There's something else that bothers me a little about the complete character study that's made before you even begin to write. Of course, know something about your character! But in real life we get to know people gradually. People reveal to us only what they want us to know. They all keep secrets, they have other lives, other interests, which to me makes people more and more intriguing as these things are discovered. Who wants to have a blueprint of every stranger as soon as they meet? I think this is the way it should be in fiction too.

A character must be consistent to his or her own nature. However, in real life, circumstances can change a person's views and temperament quite drastically, whether temporarily or permanently. (Think of the crabby old man, who may only be that way through loneliness.) This same reasoning should be applied to fiction, as long as the reactions you give your characters are always logical, and providing you give your reader knowledge of such changes. Your reader is not clairvoyant. It all comes back to motivation again, that wonderful word that should be the byword of every fiction writer.

One of the delights of a writer's life is that if you don't like a day's work, you can simply throw it into the waste-paper basket before anyone else sees it. It may depress you at the time, but it may save many a rejection! Only when you're satisfied with a page do you need to put it reverently onto the growing pile of manuscript that, eventually, with luck and talent and perseverance, will become a book.

13

The Plot Thickens

The heading of this chapter was not idly chosen. Too often, the idea that seems so brilliant in the writer's mind becomes no more than a damp squib when translated onto paper.

Escapism may be a suspect word in the mind of the literary critic, but all fiction is escapism to a greater or lesser degree. Escapism is based on reality. Even in the science-fiction plot, reality plays its part, in order to make the story believable. The reader is absorbed in a fantasy and transported into another world because of the illusion of reality the writer has created.

I said earlier that there is no single correct method to sit down and write a novel, or to construct a plot. Authors each have their own way, and each book an author writes may start from a different trigger. The flexibility of our own imagination is as important as that in the chain of the plot.

Think roughly what it is you want to say in your book. What point are you trying to make in terms of psychological character development, in the breakdown of a marriage, in political up- heaval, in medieval brutality disguised in the name of religion or court intrigue?

Have a theme in mind when you begin to consider your plot. It may be nothing more original than "good triumphs over evil", but it will keep you on the fictional road you have set out for yourself. The theme of a novel can be summed up in one sentence, however long. The plot needs the entire novel to bring the theme to life.

Pacing your story is one of the essentials of writing good fiction. How fast or how slow it will be largely depends on the story you are writing. If your characters are gentle, living out a splendidly nostalgic love story, perhaps, the pacing will be slower than that used in an action-packed thriller. Your own instincts should guide you, as will the published books you have read.

Always remember that a great deal of narrative slows the pace of a story. If this is what you want, that's fine, and it is generally desirable in a historical novel to have a good sprinkling of narrative passages. To achieve maximum movement in any novel, however, you can't beat the use of good dialogue between the characters, interspersed with short scenes to change location, describe events and so on.

When constructing your novel, give your reader some surprises. Don't make everything so predictable that there is no point in reading on. In a contemporary romance, your reader will probably know who the hero is very early on, because that's the style of these books. But never underestimate the skill of the author of contemporary romances that seem so simply written. There will still be enough conflict and tension and plot twists between hero and heroine to keep the reader intrigued, and trying to guess how the obligatory happy ending is going to be achieved. Surmising the outcome of a story does not mean that the reader will or should know its course. Compare the journey that your story will take between the covers of your book, i.e. the plot, with the course of a river.

The source of the River Severn is in northern Powys in Wales and it eventually flows magnificently into the Bristol Channel. But during that long journey of 220 miles, it meanders through Shropshire, Hereford and Worcester, Gloucestershire and Avon, and has 17 tributaries. The contemporary novel would not have as many twists and turns as that of a complex river system. The densely detailed saga or blockbuster certainly might.

I am not suggesting that the locations in your story must move through six counties or more to produce a saleable result, but that it must have shape and substance and movement in it to keep the reader's interest, as well as your own.

The story that gives a character some quest to perform, as in the example in Chapter Twelve of the Western hero hunting or being hunted by his quarry, always gives the reader a sense of involvement with the characters from the start. The reader will be curious about the background of that situation, the events leading up to the day when the story begins, and will be taking on the pseudo-role of Hank Sibley as he or she reads on. This is an opening that promises a quick-fire story, all action and movement, with plenty of scene changes and tension.

Still using that brief opening as an example, there are two aspects of it that should by now be crystal clear to you. This is an all-action story and the main character has motivation for the course that the story is going to take. Pace and motivation are therefore going to play an important part in its development.

Chapters

The chapters in a novel are not the same thing as scenes. There have been published novels that have chapters of varying lengths. There have been a few published with no chapters at all. For the new writer, it is safer to stick tc tried and tested ideas in constructing your chapters. If you start with a chapter of around 3,000–4,000 words, make the others roughly the same length, without sticking so rigidly to a word count that your imagination is stifled by it.

Begin each chapter with some interesting piece of information that moves the story along, or a sparkling line of dialogue, or a new direction for the plot. Use anything that will draw your reader quickly into this new portion of the novel: they will have paused from the previous chapter—preferably at an enticing point in the story—and may be the kind who reads a chapter a night. Alternatively this may be the kind of reader, beloved of writers, who "simply couldn't put the book down". If this is the case, chances are that what helped to make your book irresistible were the tempting chapter openings.

Whatever you do, don't open your chapters in a predictable way. Don't start every one with a description of the weather, or with dialogue, or a mass of research facts that the reader won't bother to wade through before getting onto what's happening between the characters. Any one of these is an acceptable chapter opening, but vary them and don't fill your entire book with a repetition of the first one you thought of.

Scenes form parts of chapters. Everything you write is some kind of scene, and the actual writing will become easier if you think in scenes. A chapter may only consist of one scene between hero and heroine, although generally this will become tedious. Usually there are several scenes within a chapter, not necessarily with a change of location, but by subtle plot movement or by bringing in another character whose appearance will change the mood of the first scene and ease it skilfully into the next.

There may be an abrupt transition between scenes to bring the reader up sharply and plunge the action forward, as in a historical saga, when a double-line space indicates the change of scene and sometimes a change of viewpoint.

The viewpoint question is one that bothers many new writers. It used to be that novels were told strictly from one viewpoint. This is still true of the short contemporary romance and the teenage novel. In other genres the occasional switched viewpoint is becoming more widely used.

In longer novels, both contemporary and historical, it is highly advisable to keep up the tension, to highlight the twists and turns of the plots, and to write each scene from the viewpoint of the character who will give it the most impact. This does not mean that every character you introduce will take charge of a scene. The result would be bitty and the main characters diffused. But the occasional scene through the eyes of even a minor character whose actions will change the direction of the plot and move it forward is perfectly acceptable.

My rule is to always let the reader be perfectly sure who is controlling the scene and never to let minor characters take over for too long. Also, never begin the book with a minor character so that the reader is fooled into thinking that this is the hero or heroine. Make it perfectly clear who your central character is very early on.

A little scene about pottery-making in ancient Egypt, put in as an interesting "aside" for the reader when the novel is mainly set in Greece, will not meet with editorial approval.

Remember what your characters were wearing in the last chapter and keep their lifestyles consistent. Remember the mannerisms and appearance you gave them in your character sketches (to which you should refer constantly, particularly as your "cast list" grows during the writing of your book). Don't let a petite blue-eyed blonde in Chapter One become a willowy violet-eyed brunette in Chapter Five.

Characters

In any novel, one central character should be controlling your plot. Whether you have a simple storyline in a 55,000-word book, or a complex plot with a cast of 50 or more in a blockbuster, one key character should stand out. Keep that in mind when constructing the shape of your novel. Everything of importance should either involve this character, making some difference to their lives or, bring about disaster or happiness. It should always, always, always involve your main character in conflict.

Without conflict, no novel is worth reading. This may be physical as predicted in the Hank Sibley story, or psychological as in a tense thriller, or emotional in a romance, or dramatic in a historical saga or children's adventure story. There are any number of ways to create conflict, and reading published novels will show you the various ways successful authors have tackled this part of our craft.

Show what your characters are doing and allow your readers to understand their motives by letting the characters themselves live out their scenes, rather than you telling it all in narrative form. Show, don't tell.

Never forget to link your scenes in some way. As with chapters, each should lead on from the next, or be a catalyst for those to come.

Plots

An American author defines the plot of a novel as being a chain, with the scenes as the links of that chain. She brings the characteristics of a chain into her definition: strength, flexibility, material, colour and texture. In fact, all the elements that will flesh out the plot of the novel. She also defines the sub-plot neatly. If the plot is a length of chain, the sub-plot is a thinner chain, winding around it. This thinner chain should be as long as the main one and, although of lesser importance, it must always weave in and out of the stronger chain, reinforcing and supporting it.

You can see that this analogy could apply to any number of sub-plots, by thinking of various thin chains winding around a thicker one and helping to make it stronger still. But only in a very long novel, or in a tense crime novel, perhaps, would you have several sub-plots, each contributing towards the conclusion and giving the reader a more rounded picture of the story.

Be original in building your plot. Every theme has been used before. The way you construct your plot around a well-used theme should be unique to you. You don't want a reader to begin your story and think suspiciously that it seems familiar, and then realize with fury that you've been re-writing *Gone With the Wind*. Readers will quickly lose faith in such an author. They expect to read original work.

So too, does your first reader, who will be an editor. Editors are the people who are inundated with manuscripts every day. To be successful in today's competitive market, you have to work at giving them something extra. Let your own voice be heard through the plot. This is not the same as author-intrusion, by which I mean the twee little moral utterances putting across your own point of view and holding up the story. Letting your own voice be heard in the plot means giving the book your individual interpretation of the events you describe. Make this *your* story and nobody else's. Don't copy anyone else's style. Develop your own, so that other writers will be envying yours. Discovering a new author who is completely original in approach and style is every editor's dream.

No author really wants to be compared with another. It may be flattering, but it's also typecasting. To be the first, original, Amelia Smithers is far preferable to being the new write-alike Felicity Moore.

Path, Length, Obstacles and Time-span, all make up the elements of your book, and the initial letters of these form the word PLOT.

The path is the direction your story is going to take. You have choices to make when you begin a novel—there are many directions in which your characters can go. You may discard the first path you think of, realizing that it will lead nowhere; another path may be too narrow, giving the characters little scope for movement or action and restricting them; yet another may be too complicated, beset with too many pitfalls, so that the characters would get lost long before the story was resolved.

It may take you some time to find the right path for your characters to take. They may begin on one path and have to be turned back, which means that you must start all over again. If you want to get your plot development right, if you want to write the best book that you can and get it published, you will do so.

The length of the novel will guide the way you construct your plot and also the way you allow your characters to behave. In a blockbuster novel, character development can be more detailed and leisurely. In a short novel, characterization must be crisper and more sharply defined. At some stage during the writing your characters will develop lives of their own, and in some magical way they will become very real to you.

This may not happen all at once, but when it does you may be tempted to let your imagination run riot, involving them in all kinds of escapades that may border on the ridiculous. As opposed to the sub-plot, in which other characters are involved, this is the author indulging in sideline interludes that hold up the main action. All this will affect the proposed length and balance of your book.

Obstacles must come into every plot. The story that moves smoothly from A to Z with no obstacles to confuse things, is a pointless and dreary exercise. It is not a novel. Novels are filled with obstacles for the protagonists to overcome. This strengthens their characters, fills readers with admiration and adds to their enjoyment of the book.

If the movement in your book starts to flag, ask yourself if this is the time to present a new obstacle to the reader, perhaps through a new character who will continue to be important to the plot, or through any number of external circumstances. A few chosen at random could be weather conditions—a plane grounded by fog; a storm blowing up at sea; rain-swollen roads;

or blistering heat in the desert. Or you could introduce a mechanical device that is temporarily out of order, badly affecting your characters—the broken telephone cable; the camera that failed to record some vital evidence; the telex that didn't deliver a message; the loss of electrical power to a life-support machine; a jammed lift; or a faulty engine in a plane/ship/car.

There are limitless ways to pep up a flagging scene. The essential thing is to make whatever means you use perfectly logical, however surprising. There must be no possibility of letting the reader suspect that you put this scene in because you didn't know where to go next. The experienced author will insert pointers in the preceding scenes, if necessary (it isn't always), so that the reader is not left sceptical instead of marvelling at the author's ingenuity.

But you didn't know until you reached this point that such events were going to happen? If you want to make them stick, and you need those pointers, I'm afraid it's revision time again.

The time-span is not the same as its length. Decide before you begin to construct your plot, just how much time your book is going to cover, be it hours or months or years. Many people don't consider this, but if you do so at the outset, you will automatically have some parameters in which to manoeuvre your characters, setting, background and so on. You will know where your book is going to begin and the approximate place where it will end.

If your book has a one-year setting, you may think it's worth letting the changing seasons play a prominent role in your story. If your book is a generational saga, then at the very least you will know the age of your main character when it begins, and how much of his or her life you intend to expand upon. If your book starts with a child of eight years old, and ends with the same character as a matriarch of 80, you will know that your book must cover 72 years, with all the necessary research that that will entail.

In a thriller, time may be an essential factor. Your characters may have just 12 hours to break some vital international code before the balloon goes up. By knowing you only have a 12-hour time-span before you begin your book, you will have something to work towards.

127

Think of your plot as a graph: you begin at an interesting point to intrigue the reader; and you write scenes that create growing suspense in a series of waves, giving your readers time to pause now and then by slowing down the action just a little. Never so much that they lose interest, but enough to let them take breath and not expire. Keep those waves on your graph progressing higher and higher until you reach the climax of the book, which must be exciting, moving, emotional, or hilarious—whatever fits the tone of your book. This point should always be explanatory. Don't leave your reader high and dry up there with no logical explanation of what it was all about.

Constructing a plot can also be compared with making a tower with children's building blocks. There is a solid base when you need a lot of blocks to make the thing balance, but gradually you can use fewer and fewer as the top ones take up the shape, until finally the pinnacle stands alone. Your pyramid is complete. Your book is finished. The more you write, the more skilled you will become—as long as you keep on writing, or you will just be left with a heap of blocks.

A plot consists of everything you want to say in your book. Beware of the myth that some things do not make good plots. You may hear it said that you should avoid this theme or that, or a particular publishing house is no longer looking at certain settings. This may well be so—for a time.

Trends come and go in fiction, and what is out this year may well be in next. So don't despair. If you want to use a certain theme badly enough, use it. If it doesn't sell right away, shelve it for the time being, bring it out at some future date, dust it off, and either send it out again or revise it completely when you've had a chance to look at it objectively.

And remember, anything that is good enough will sell.

14

Business Matters Arising

There are various matters that arise in the course of a writer's "apprenticeship" that may need clarifying. Some are legal points, some are merely the accepted professional way of conducting your business. Some will just be things you have vaguely heard about, and are wondering if they are for you. Since you are now a one-man-band, you should be aware of them.

Rights

You own the *copyright* on your own original work. When you send away an article or short story for publication, you will write on the cover-sheet the words *First British Serial Rights offered*. This does not mean you are offering a 2,000-word story to be used as a serial. It is just one of the peculiarities of publishing jargon and simply means you are stating that this is a story that hasn't been published before, and that you are offering this particular magazine the right to publish it first.

If you are submitting an article or story to an American or Canadian magazine, you would put on the cover sheet the words *First North American Rights offered*. The editor concerned will know exactly what is meant.

There is no need to put this declaration on poems or very short pieces of work, unless in the case of articles you intend to offer them abroad after they have been published here, or vice versa. It is very unwise to offer the same article to a second British magazine when it has already been published, without making absolutely clear what rights you are offering. Editors

129

don't look kindly on this practice and may not buy your work again.

However, you may offer them *Second British Serial Rights*, which will let them know that this piece has been published before. Some magazines will take Second Rights. Many won't. Some will only consider them after a period of years has elapsed between the first appearance of the article or story and the second. Your payment is usually less for a second printing, but it all depends on the publisher. Also, if a period of years has elapsed, inflation may have increased the payment rate considerably, so you may do quite well out of Second Rights. It is also courteous, and may be requested, to let the second publisher know the name of the first one who published your work.

Anything that has been published in magazine form here can be offered abroad, with the same proviso. If you are offering First North American Rights, always put on the cover-sheet that the article/story was first published in whichever British magazine bought it. Then the editor, and you, will know exactly where you both stand.

When you offer the manuscript of a novel to a publisher, you do not need to say that you are offering First British Serial Rights, or FBSR for short. It is becoming acceptable to offer copies of the same novel manuscript to several publishers if you wish, and if more than one of them likes your book, you will then decide which offer to take for it. Once you have accepted an offer, write to the others asking for your manuscript's return, and telling them it is now going to be published by so-and-so.

It is unlikely that any publisher is going to "steal" your work and publish it under another name. If you wish to take every precaution, deposit another copy with your bank or solicitor with all details, witnessed and dated. Do the same with your offering letter from your chosen publisher and your formal acceptance letter of his terms. In the ghastly event of a thwarted publisher saying he is going to publish your book when you've already accepted another offer, you will at least have legal backing that he is not at liberty to go ahead.

Contracts

Contracts are not normally sent to writers for articles or short stories. A letter from the editor with the offer of a fee, and your return letter of acceptance is usually all that happens, to be followed in due course by the cheque. This will sometimes be on receipt of your letter, or on publication of the work, depending on each publication's system, and allowing for any end-of-the-month accounting.

When a publisher offers to buy your full-length book, they will offer you a sum of money in advance of publication. If this seems reasonable to you, you will accept their terms and reply accordingly. The publisher's letter should also state the royalty percentages, which are usually $7\frac{1}{2}$ % of each copy sold once the book has earned out its advance. This figure varies between publishers, and will often go up to 10 % or more when a certain number of copies have been sold.

Having agreed to these terms, you will then receive a contract. Study it very carefully. Much of the wording will be obscure—not at all like the book that has just been accepted!—and it will be full of legal terminology. Much of it will be quite straightforward. You will know that the advance is assured, the royalty terms stated—including the percentages due to you if the original publisher makes any further sales of your book in large-print, paperback, foreign editions, special library editions, book-club sales and so on. You will be told that you will receive a number of complimentary copies of your book on publication—usually six in this country, considerably more from US publishers. You will be given the approximate date of publication which can be very flexible. The contract will also state that the publisher wishes to take out an option on your next book or your next two books under the name you are using on the first book.

There are many other paragraphs to read. If you are unhappy about any of them, take them to someone with experience in deciphering legal contracts before you sign it. The Society of Authors has its own legal department which will do this for its members. Address for further details—84 Drayton Gardens, London SW10 9SD. Or see your own solicitor, or an established author who may be able to help.

Agents

A *literary agent* will take care of any contract queries for you. Whether you acquire the services of an agent is entirely up to you. Some writers say they couldn't exist without them, leaning on them to take on all the business chores and leaving them free to get on with the writing. There are inevitable delays between you sending your manuscript to an agent, and the agent then reading it, making any appropriate suggestions on its improvement, and then sending it on to a publisher.

Other writers enjoy being part of it all, even to haggling with publishers and trying to get their money out of them, which is not always as forthcoming as many would like.

There are pros and cons regarding acquiring an agent and it is up to each author to make up his or her own mind. An agent will generally get you a larger advance than you could get for yourself. But then you have to pay the agent 10% of all your earnings. And you still have to wait for the advance to be earned out of book sales before you start to get any royalties. So the large advance, although wonderful at the time, also means that you have to wait longer before you get any royalties.

Since every publisher presumably wants to get as much mileage as possible out of every book taken on, and outlines all such possible avenues, as mentioned above in your contract, a publisher also acts as an agent to some extent.

Unfortunately, it can be difficult to get a literary agent to take you on nowadays unless you already have a track record of published work. You may be lucky in finding one. The *Writers' & Artists Yearbook* lists a number of them, or you may find one through a writer-friend or one of the writers' organizations, or by attending a writers' conference or weekend where like-minded people will give you moral support and friendship.

Support Groups

The Writers' Summer School is held annually at Swanwick in Derbyshire, every August. It lasts six days, covers all aspects of writing, and has been an enormous help to both new and experienced writers. Details (with SAE) can be obtained from the secretary, Mrs Philippa Boland, The Red House, Marden Hill, Crowborough, Sussex TN6 1XN.

This is only one of a host of various writing events to be found throughout the country. Details of others can be found in writers' magazines, through writers' circles, or sometimes posted in libraries, or through local WEA information at colleges.

Writers' Circles exist in most towns. There is a published book listing those in this country. For details, write to Jill Dick, Oldacre, Horderns Park Road, Chapel-en-le-Frith, Derbyshire SK12 68Y (with SAE).

Writers' magazines give a great deal of information and articles by and for writers, with news of books, fiction and non-fiction, and markets at home and overseas. *Writers' Monthly* magazine is an excellent example. There are also weekend seminars organized by the same team. Details of both from the Contributing Editor, Alison Gibbs, 3 Crawford House, 132 North Street, St Andrews, Fife, Scotland KY16 9AF (with SAE).

Organizations for every type of writer exist. The Romantic Novelists' Association and the Crime Writers' Association are just two. There is also the Children's Writers' Group, PEN International, The Penman Club, The Poetry Society, Poet's Workshop, The Radiowriters Association, and others. Details of these and more can be found in the *Writers' & Artists' Yearbook*.

Pen-Names

The use of *pen-names* worries some new writers. How do you get one? Why have one at all? Is it necessary? You get one simply by choosing whatever name you want to call yourself for your writing career. Some people prefer to keep their private life separate from their business one.

The elderly lady you meet at the hairdresser's on OAP days may not want to be recognized as being Delphine Delovely, steamy romantic novelist extraordinaire . . . Chuck Waggoner, the latest bestselling gun-totin' beer-swillin' Western author may not want everyone to know that in reality he's mild-mannered Ronnie Potts of Milton Keynes . . . (no, I've got nothing against Milton Keynes). It may be embarrassing to them because of their quiet personalities. It may be that they use more than one pen-name because they are prolific enough to write for several publishers, perhaps producing different types of novels. This is another reason for having pen-names.

Is it necessary to have one? It may be, if you do write for different publishers. When you sign that contract (see above) and agree to give your publisher the option on your next book, and you are also signing away the name that will be on the book—for the term of the option. So, apart from the glow it will give you to think that this publisher wants your next book as well . . . remember that they are being canny too. If the first book is a hit, your publisher has the option on your next.

If the publisher eventually turns down your option book you are free to offer it to someone else. If you then work happily with a new publisher, you can continue using your original name without thinking up a new one.

All this is where the services of an agent can be of help, if you really want to keep to one name. He or she can do any arguing and negotiating for you with the publisher, and the outcome will depend on them. If you're not averse to a bit of verbal arm-twisting, you may do it all equally as well by yourself.

Public Lending Right

Public Lending Right will feature in your life as soon as you have published a book, whether fiction or non-fiction. Don't ignore it, or think that with only one published book to your credit you are small fry. You are not. You're as eligible as anyone to register for PLR, and you should do so as soon as your book is published. Write to the Public Lending Right Office, Bayheath Road, Prince Regent Street, Stockton-On-Tees, Cleveland TS18 1DF for a registration form.

What PLR means in practical terms is that every registered author whose books are in public libraries will receive a sum of money in mid-February. All editions of the books, as long as they are in British libraries, should be included. The amount the author receives will depend on the number of books they have published, on the library selection (a number of libraries take part, being changed every few years, and the numbers of borrowed books are calculated countrywide), and on the current amount allowed by the government for the scheme. You must apply before the end of June for your books to be included in the next year's accounting and thereafter.

PLR has proved extremely valuable to authors. All the editions of each book count as a separate entry and will have their own ISBN number, which is entered on the form. (You will be told exactly what to do, so don't worry about the technical terms.) My own annual print-out of the various editions of my books now runs to a third page.

In the 1985–1986 print-out, one of my contemporary romances, *The Kissing Time* (Jean Saunders) was borrowed an estimated 28,000 times, bringing me £350·28. One of my historical novels, *The Savage Moon* (Rowena Summers) was borrowed an estimated 23,000 times, bringing me £290·64.

Common sense will tell you that not all books are in all libraries, so if yours doesn't happen to be in any of those chosen for calculation, there is nothing to be earned on it in that particular year. Which is why the libraries used are changed regularly, to give everyone a fair chance.

Tax

Now for something not quite so nice, but which has to be dealt with sooner or later: *Income Tax*. When you write for profit, you are liable for income tax payments. When your earnings become taxable, according to current earnings-allowance figures, it is well worthwhile getting the advice of an accountant who will tell you all the things that can be offset against your earnings. These may well surprise you.

All of the following can be claimed by a writer who can show that he is making money from his writing: pens; pencils; typing paper; carbon paper; photocopying expenses; photographs needed for your work (whether to illustrate articles or for publicity purposes); headed notepaper to advertise your status; business cards; all postage incurred in your work; subscriptions to relevant magazines to aid with your work, or for market study; and research books used for the same purpose.

You can also claim travel expenses, providing you are using the journeys for business purposes and not solely for pleasure (in the case of holiday trips for which the research angle is incidental, a proportion of the expenses may be claimed); telephone rental charges and a fair fraction of your annual calls; the cost of an answering machine; a proportion of your home running-costs; and car expenses used in the course of your work. Certain entertaining of visiting editors and/or agents may also be an acceptable claim.

Attendances at writers' conferences, seminars, meetings of any writers' organizations to which you may belong and subscriptions to the same can be claimed, together with expenses incurred in travelling and any necessary meals.

If you become involved in a lot of public speaking about your work, it is reasonable to claim for a certain number of hairdressing and clothes expenses, if you can show that this is above normal. The amount allowed may not be very high. You cannot expect to claim for every new jumper and pair of jeans that you would be wearing to the shops anyway. The argument is that you will wear the new clothes you bought especially for a TV appearance at many more functions later, so you can only expect to claim a reasonable amount for its purchase. You may argue back that you had to spend the money on the clothes in the first place, but be reasonable in all such dealings.

In all the above, you will be required to give clear details and receipts, to your accountant for submitting to the tax inspector.

Don't forget the purchase of a typewriter, or word processor and printer equipment and accessories. These will come under Capital Allowances, but your accountant will sort the details out for you. If you are sending your claims to the tax inspector yourself, list such large items separately. If you are still in doubt, you can always request an interview with the tax inspector. They are there to help (honestly).

A video recorder may be a necessity in recording certain programmes to help with your research. You will need to buy cassettes for this purpose—claim them too.

If your work involves interviewing people, you may find the expense of a video camera worth your while, and certainly a tape recorder and a good quality camera. Don't forget to claim for the films and the processing. Providing you can assure the tax inspector that this is used in connection with your work, he or she will look sympathetically on your claim for its purchase.

Always keep receipts for anything you buy in connection with your work, including stamps for the Post Office. The costs incurred in submitting many pieces of work during the course of a year is very high. Including the stamped, addressed envelopes expected from publishers, the cost of your manuscript submissions can run into many pounds. Submitting to overseas publishers can send your bill skywards. With these, send International Reply Coupons to cover return postage, disregarding a return envelope.

If you use professional services such as those of a literary agent, publicity agent, typing or secretarial services, all these expenses are deductable. So are visits to theatres and so on in the cause of research. Always make it clear when claiming such things what the reasons were for including the items. It will save many letters passing to and fro, which will harrass you, and make the tax inspector edgy.

If you have someone to clean your house while you're writing, those expenses are allowed. In fact, anything you do that furthers your work interests can reasonably be claimed against tax. If you are an article-writer, or a fiction-writer, don't you often use items found in the daily newspaper for new ideas of your own? Therefore newspapers can be deduced to be a valid claim on your tax form.

Always be courteous and sensible when making your claims. Anything nonsensical and outrageous will only annoy the tax inspector and probably result in your being investigated and gaining nothing.

When you are earning over a government-specified figure, you will be eligible for *Value Added Tax* (VAT). The amount you are allowed to earn before paying this tax is usually announced on Budget Day, but your accountant will advise you and tell you what to do about it. If you don't have an accountant —and by the time you are earning anything approaching VAT figures you certainly should have—contact the nearest VAT office (details in your phone book). When you near the necessary earning figure is the correct time to do so, not a year or so later. You will then be assigned your own VAT inspector. It is a thought that horrifies many people, who until now, may not have realized that their writing puts them into the class of self-employed.

Briefly, when you reach the higher earning range, which at the present time is in the region of £20,000, you reclaim all the VAT you pay on everything to do with your writing business, including stationery, telephone bills, typewriters and so on. You are given your own VAT number, and you must then obtain a special VAT receipt for everything you buy. This word will figure largely in your life from now on. In effect, you charge the seller the VAT incurred, and then claim it back via Customs and Excise through a process of paperwork.

I do not intend to go into more detail here, nor do I profess to understand all the working of it. To explain the intricacies of VAT needs someone with expert knowledge and there are plenty of people able to give you all the help and advice you want. But be aware that it must be done, and do it when it becomes necessary. Good luck.

15

My Favourite Things

This is a chapter of odds and ends, of things I've read heard or experienced. It's the sort of chapter I love to read in other writers' manuals. And no, this is not an original idea. The words in it are. After all that hard work in the previous chapters and the shock of realizing that the tax inspector will take an interest in you as well as the occasional fans with their heady adulation, it's time for some fun.

But this chapter is not *just* for fun. You, like me, will hopefully be reminded of things you thought you had forgotten and, in turn, your writer's imagination will be stimulated—that's what it's all about.

Some of the things that writers find fascinating may be incomprehensible to anyone else. But then, we wouldn't be wildly interested in the finer details of a plumber's day or a photographic model's schedule, would we? (Unless we were writing an article on a plumber or a model, of course. . . .)

There are many things that interest me. Like the solid chain that is my writing, I love all the little thinner chains that weave in and out of it and make up the entire panorama of my writing world. It is essentially the world of books, of finding things out, of wonderful friendships that may begin and end over a weekend conference but have nevertheless touched my life and made it richer. It is never boring.

Every human brain is a wonderful computer, with the capacity to store snippets of information, from the essential to the trivial. It can bring memory into play at unexpected moments; it can be forced into remembering long-forgotten incidents; it is a writer's best friend.

Every writer becomes a collector. Not only of pamphlets, cuttings, photographs, travel brochures, and the hundred and one things that might be useful in an article or story someday. The writer also becomes a collector of quotes, overheard conversations, definitions, favourite words and phrases.

We collect crazy things too. Do you know what an "eponym" is? The brainier among you will, of course. I didn't, until I discovered that it is a most delightful addition to the writer's vocabulary. It means a word derived from someone's name that has now been accepted into everyday language. I came across some wonderful ones relating to the writing business. Are they true or false? I have my doubts about one or two and I don't pretend to know the answer. For me, the fun of them lies in the telling.

Hiram B. Hype was a well-known American PR man. Phineas T. Barnum was a renowned showman. Hiram persuaded Barnum to paint the sides of one of his elephants with a garish slogan advertising a salacious novel, which thus became the first book to be Hyped. . . .

The Booker Prize is one of our most prestigious literary awards. In the 1930s there was a little-known American jazz musician with the splendid name of Booker T. Prizewinner. How, or why, or if it was his name that came to be adopted for the annual event, nobody seems to know. Curiouser and curiouser. . . .

Ever heard of Big John Bestseller? He was the patriarch of a Dallas-based publishing company. He was known to his people as Number One. Hence the phrase Number One Bestseller, which apparently appeared on the cover of every book he published.

Jacobus Index (circa 1446–1502) was a so-called Italian scribe and half-wit. (Do the two go together?) How his name came to be adopted for the index of a book is a mystery, since he was such a duffer he couldn't get the order of the alphabet into his head, no matter how hard he tried.

A more home-grown eponym came with Mabel Potboiler. She was a Gloucestershire spinster, who was reputedly a hugely successful romantic novelist. (No, I hadn't heard of her either.) But then, she was supposed to have had 152 pen-names and written more than 3,000 novels. She died in obscurity, leaving her tabby-cat the wealthiest in England.

I didn't say they were all true! I can't vouch for any of them. I just read them and stored them away in my head, because they amused me so much. To me, they're little gems to lighten a writer's day when the words won't come and writers' block has set in. (Yes, we all get those days.)

Additional reading

There are many helpful books for writers. Dipping into any of them is like meeting an old friend who understand the despairs and delights of our craft. As well as the various research books I have mentioned in other chapters, those below are ones that I have particularly enjoyed and can recommend for your own reading.

The Craft of Novel Writing by Dianne Doubtfire (Allison & Busby)

Teach Yourself Creative Writing by Dianne Doubtfire (Hodder & Stoughton)

How to Write Stories for Magazines by Donna Baker (Allison & Busby)

To Writers With Love by Mary Wibberley (Buchan & Enright)

Dear Author by Michael Legat (Pelham Books)

Writing for Pleasure and Profit by Michael Legat (Robert Hale)

How to Publish Your Poetry by Peter Finch (Allison & Busby)

Writing Juvenile Stories and Novels by Phyllis Whitney (The Writer Inc.)

The Making of a Novelist by Margaret Thomson Davis (Allison & Busby)

Becoming a Writer by Dorothea Brand (Papermac)

Low-Cost Word-Processing by Gordon Wells (Allison & Busby)

The Magazine Writer's Handbook by Gordon Wells (Allison & Busby)

Research for Writers by Ann Hoffman (A. & C. Black)

An Author's Handbook by David Bolt (Judy Piatkus)

The Way to Write Short Stories by Michael Baldwin (Elm Tree Books)

Successful Freelance Journalism by Fay Goldie (Oxford University Press)

Writing a Thriller by André Jute (A. & C. Black)

Writing Crime Fiction by H. R. F. Keating (A. & C. Black)

The Craft of Writing Romance by Jean Saunders (Allison & Busby)

Quotes

I love other people's quotes. Some can be cynical, clever, funny, ghastly. This one is attributed to W.C. Fields. When asked if he liked children, he replied, "Yes—boiled."

While you're still grimacing, get your writing brain working. Despite the sentiments, it's a masterly bit of characterization in no more than two words. Put a similar type of statement into a fictional character's mouth and your reader will hate him immediately! (Make sure that's what you intend. . . .)

Another quote, from a nineteenth-century theorist, referred rather grandly to the monarchy, but I think it can be applied just as well to any kind of fiction: "Its mystery is its life. We must not let in daylight upon magic."

Book jackets are some of my favourite things. They're more salacious than they used to be, wouldn't you say? But some of those old titles were suggestive enough in their day. *The Wandering Beauty, The Unhappy Mistake, The Unfortunate Bride* and *The Dumb Virgin* were all written by a lady called Aphra Behn. She was the first woman novelist in Britain, and those titles were published in 1687.

Aphra Behn was also the first woman to have a stage-play produced. It was called *The Forced Marriage, or the Jealous*

Bridegroom. (Do those compute?) The play ran for six days at the Duke's Theatre in London in 1670.

I would love to have met Aphra Behn. It was said that her works were noted for the "robustness of their dialogue, and the indelicacy of the situations portrayed." Obviously a lady well ahead of her time in writing terms!

As writers of the 1980s we tend to think we're coining new phrases and situations all the time. Not a bit of it. Consider this—which gave one or two people palpitations at one writers' conference where I quoted it, until All Was Revealed:

> *Good God,* what a night that was,
> The bed was so soft, and how we clung,
> Burning together, lying this way and that,
> Our uncontrollable passions flowing.

Was it penned by the steamy poet-of-the-week at the local writers' circle? Well, no. It was written by a scribe by the name of Petronius Arbiter in the 1st century, AD.

This is part of a contemporary poem that I admire very much, because the stark simplicity of the words sums up all the emotion that is so understated, but none the less real. The poem is called *Who?* by Adrian Henri, and this is the last part of it:

> You say we don't get on any more—
> But who can I laugh on beaches with, wondering at the
> noise the limpets make still sucking in the tide—
> Who can I buy my next Miles Davis record to share with—
> Who makes coffee the way I like it—
> and love, the way I used to like it—
> who came in from the sun, the day the world went spinning
> away from me—
> who doesn't wash the clothes I always want—
> who spends my money—
> who wears my dressing-gown and always leaves the sleeves
> turned up—
> who makes me feel as empty as the house does when she's
> not there—
> who else but you.

143

I'm not a poet, except in a very modest way, but poetry has always meant a lot to me and I think it does to every writer, especially fiction writers.

Songs

Song lyrics, too, can stir the heart in many ways, evoking a mood, an era, a time of pleasure or happiness or sorrow or magic . . . so many things. I only have to hear some song titles to be transported immediately into an instant world of my imagination. My tastes are varied and not highbrow. The following titles all evoke memories, but I'm not going to tell you just why they, or their lyrics or their music, mean something to me!

Days of Wine and Roses
Pavane For a Dead Princess
Roses of Picardy
I'll See You in my Dreams
Unforgettable
The Very Thought of You
The Last Time I Felt Like This
Barcarolle, from Tales of Hoffmann
You are my Sunshine
Solveig's Song from Peer Gynt
Jesu, Joy of Man's Desiring
The Skeleton in the Cupboard
Softly Awakes my Heart, from Samson and Delilah
Scarborough Fair
Plaisir D'Amour
Song of India
The Donkey Serenade
Jean (sung by Rod McKuen)
Autumn Leaves
Jerusalem
My Blue Heaven
Spanish Eyes
Moonglow

144

The Skye Boat Song
Waltzing Matilda

And on and on . . . I would be no good as a contender for Desert Island Discs. The island would need to be as big as Hawaii (and preferably it would be Hawaii).

Anecdotes

I love anecdotes. This little story was told to me recently by a writer friend. One of the members at her writers' circle used to bring her dog to meetings. As the woman couldn't hear very well, she and her dog always sat at the front of the hall. This was fine, except when the invited speaker was boring or went on too long. The audience still listened politely but not the dog, who always showed his feelings by giving a loud yawn at the most embarrassing moment. Speakers, be warned.

Since this is a fun and work chapter combined—oh, you didn't realize I was brainwashing you into thinking for yourself? Don't tell me you aren't compiling your own list of song titles by now, for a start! (I promise you, it gets addictive.) Anyway, since this is a fun and work chapter combined. . . .

Many a starting-point for stories, articles or novels has been personal experience. This is one of mine. It concerns Japanese tourists. I have nothing against the Japanese, honestly. This is not a racist book. I'm sure they have their own impressions of the British tourist! But just as every race has its own peculiarities, they become more marked when they're abroad. (In fact, I'm thinking of writing a book called The Tourist Abroad.)

I don't think there are any Japanese in Japan. They're all living in Greyhound buses touring America. They all start out with an extra appendage over one arm—it's called a camera. When they emerge from their buses, they form into instant groups for photo sessions. By now, the poor courier is carrying their bundle of cameras, using each one in turn to photograph the group, so that each has his own personal record. (No, *photographic* record, silly. Oh well. . . .)

145

At a well-known tourist spot, the tourists emerge again and mass into instant group formation for the official photo. This time the courier leaps out with a prepared signboard announcing Japanese Tour, Grand Canyon 1984, or whatever. (Believe me, it happened!) Precision is second nature to them. So is the exaggerated politeness that is part of the Japanese character.

We met one group at the Grand Canyon. The air on the plateau is thin, the height above the canyon dizzying. One of the Japanese ladies on the next tour bus to ours became ill with palpitations. The group clustered around her protectively until it was a wonder she could breathe at all and then the paramedics came screaming along the road in their ambulance, all lights flashing, just like in a TV soap opera.

The lady soon recovered with the help of some oxygen. Until then, the group had been very self-contained. For some reason I caught her eye and felt obliged to ask if she was feeling better. Suddenly, it was if I was the star guest at a party. The woman smiled and nodded. Thirty other Japanese smiled and nodded. Thirty-one Japanese tourists bowed to my husband and me, and thirty-one gleaming Japanese smiles seemed to follow us around for the rest of the day.

Now what does all this have to do with writing? Not much. Except that if I ever decide to put a Japanese character in one of my books I shall remember that incident. I remember it now and it still brings a smile. Perhaps they too, may remember that not all British tourists are stiff-upper-lipped, and that there's something to be said for us jolly good fellows after all.

Cities

A strange word to include in a writer's pot-pourri of favourite things? Not for me. I only have to hear the name of a city, a village, or any remembered place, and my mind begins working at once. I taste the heat of Tunisia, remember the power of Niagara Falls, feel humbled by that awesome Grand Canyon. A sense of place can have an enormous effect on a writer, if you let it. My list is a dozen favourites, large and small, and all have their own imagery for me. These are personal memories and ideas that will let you see a little of what I see when I hear their names.

London: excitement; pea-souper fog; pageantry; my birthplace; the blitz; publishers; meeting Dirk Bogarde; Oxford Street; tea at the Ritz; the tale my mother told me of Queen Mary saying what a sweet baby I was (she always swore it was true); a certain dinner-cruise on the Thames; writers' meeting-places; being photographed with Barbara Cartland.

Paris: the Louvre Museum, especially the wonderful Egyptian section; Versailles; Montmartre by night; the beautiful church of Sacre Coeur; the sound of guitars; the flowers in the Tuilleries; French bread; the language and gesticulations; car-honkers; frites; hot chestnuts; and the old men playing petanque.

Indian Queens: an evocative name for a small village in Cornwall. I just love the name. I've no idea how it got it.

Mildura, Australia: where my emigrant uncle lived, and where I had a wonderful holiday, meeting my aunt and a host of cousins, and realized that I have more Aussie relatives than British ones. Good on you, sports.

New York: the Statue of Liberty, seen at night from the air, like a little green goddess in the ocean; publishers; The Tavern on the Green in Central Park, followed by a horse-drawn carriage-ride; exotic Chinatown; walking around the top of the Empire State Building, and knowing how King Kong felt.

Summercourt . . . and some are not. A silly family joke said every time we drive through the little Cornish village.

Hong Kong: the real thing; junks on the river; The view of the fabulous harbour from the Peak; but, most of all, the gorgeous doe-eyed Chinese children in their identical outfits, trailing round dutifully after their teachers; the night market—the poor man's nightclub—where you can bargain for anything, and everything's a bargain; sleazy back-streets; and afternoon tea at the Peninsula Hotel alongside the odd sheik or two.

The Isle of Skye: beautiful, misty mornings and glorious sunsets; evocative of Prince Charles Stuart, the Bonnie Prince Charlie; a place essentially for romantics.

Rotorua: sulphur smells; Incredible mud pools, geysers and

hot springs; the glorious Maori dancers; the fantastic motel where we stayed with our own private outdoor hot spa pool; the sheep, the small hillocks, and more sheep; the wild lupins and yellow gorse; and more sheep.

Crete: blistering heat; Magnificent Greek amphitheatres and ancient geological sites; Dizzying roads around the mountains; a farmer efficiently ploughing with equipment reminiscent of that used in biblical days; the verdant plain of windmills high amongst the mountains; the blue, blue sea, as clear as crystal; smiling waiters and wonderful moussaka; and Greek dancing in the open air around a still lake.

Jersey: the chilling German underground hospital; the attractive proximity to England and France; seeing Bergerac being filmed on the beach; sea-food restaurants; a cosy little hotel away from it all; and Lillie Langtry's grave.

Las Vegas: everything that's big and brash about America; spectacular hotels and casinos and marvellous, marvellous shows; also, the Liberace Museum, an incredible collection of memorabilia, clothes and artefacts and pianos, and an unusual insight into a star performer's life.

That's my collection of memorable places. It's only a tiny portion of those stored away in my head, to bring out on rainy days and remember with pleasure. Who said that travel doesn't broaden the mind?

Oh, and there's just one more place that was far more than a mere location. The SS *Queen Mary*, now a floating hotel at Long Beach, California, where I once attended a conference organized by the Romance Writers of America. The *Queen Mary* is still, and will always be, essentially British. Nothing can take that aura away from her, despite the officers and cabin crew and restaurant staff who take you by surprise when they suddenly start speaking in American accents. The old British telephone box is still on deck, the museum part houses models of all the great British ships of the century, and there is undoubtedly a feeling of pride in the enduring Britishness of the ship.

While we were there for those memorable few days, a Hawaiian wedding took place on board. Even more spectacular was one of those High School Proms I've only ever seen in

Hollywood movies. I always suspected that they didn't really exist and were invented by the film industry. But they're real. In America, where anything can happen, they're alive and well and thriving.

It was unbelievably exciting to see the college girls arriving in their ballgowns, all looking like Scarlett O'Hara in *Gone With the Wind*, the young men in their white tailsuits and white shoes and gloves, and totally unselfconscious of the effect they were having on everyone else. Perhaps it was only the few British writers there who took any real notice, anyway, but it was certainly a memory I cherish.

Occasionally, we all make a statement in public of which we're modestly pleased. When I was chairperson of a panel at another writers' conference, someone asked what value such a conference was to each writer on the panel. The answers were as expected from those who know from experience the help and support to be gained from new friends and old, to say nothing of the contact with editors and publishers, the excitement of meeting well-known writers/speakers, getting news of markets, and stimulating workshops. On being pressed, I added this:

> For those few days I am no longer just my husband's wife (and I love him very much); I am no longer just my children's mother (and I love them very much); I am no longer just my grandchildren's Nanny (and I love all seven of them very much). For those few days, I am *me*; I'm a person with a unique identity, and that's the greatest value of a writers' conference to me.

This sentiment applies to any gathering of writers. When you have been to a conference or to any small meeting in someone's home, you will know exactly what I mean. If people ask you what it was like, and you suddenly realize you have the same feelings that I expressed, you may quote me, no charge.

*   *   *

149

Finally, dear writer, I will leave you with my two favourite quotes involving one very special word. I wish you all the luck in the world in achieving it for yourself.

Success is what happens when something goes right.
Success often comes from not knowing your limitations.

THE CRAFT OF WRITING ROMANCE
Jean Saunders

Starting with the typical "beginners' questions", Jean Saunders goes on to show how to plan the structure of a romance, build convincing characters, open chapters and write a love scene. She explains how to do the research which gives a historical or contemporary romance its authenticity, and she gives advice on submitting manuscripts and surviving rejection. There are also two invaluable chapters in which the top editors and the most successful authors — among them Barbara Cartland, Sarah Harrison and Claire Rayner — offer their advice to the beginner.

WRITERS' QUESTIONS ANSWERED
Gordon Wells

In *Writers' Questions Answered* Gordon Wells provides answers to more than a hundred of the questions about writers and writing most frequently asked at writers' groups, conferences and weekend schools. This book is aimed at the beginner, but will also be useful to the writer experienced in one genre, who is about to embark on writing in another.

HOW TO PUBLISH YOURSELF
Peter Finch

How to Publish Yourself is a practically-minded guide to going it alone which covers every aspect of the enterprise from start to finish. The book also contains two invaluable appendices with lists of books and organisations which will be of interest to self-publishers, and a comprehensive bibliography and index.

THE CRAFT OF WRITING ARTICLES
Gordon Wells

The Craft of Writing Articles is the perfect guide to an enjoyable, paying hobby. It is crammed with sound practical advice and useful tips about the whole business of writing articles, from choosing and researching a subject to presentation and salesmanship.

Whatever you may wish to write about, from cookery to stamp-collecting, from photography to bizarre, local customs, the same basic guidelines apply. And these are covered in a series of short, informative chapters.

Allison & Busby Writers' Guides
Published by W. H. Allen & Co Plc

THE CRAFT OF NOVEL-WRITING

Dianne Doubtfire

Talent can't be taught, but craftsmanship certainly can. This book, written mainly with the beginner in mind, is designed to help anyone with talent and dedication to master the techniques of writing a novel which should satisfy not only the author but the reader and publisher as well. It is a clearly-written guide covering all aspects of the craft and answering many questions which confront the novice. It also contains a wealth of quotations from contemporary writers.

"Eminently practical" – Francis King, *Sunday Telegraph*

"Most unquestionably useful"—Harriet Gilbert, *Time Out*

"Succinct, clear and sensible"—*The Author*

"I would recommend it to all aspiring writers"—Jean Plaidy

"An excellent and commonsense book"—*Cosmopolitan*

"Page after page of sound practical advice . . . any novelist or would-be novelist who doesn't buy a copy of this book immediately is either arrogant or already living in a tax-haven" – *Writers' News*

HOW TO PUBLISH YOUR POETRY

Peter Finch

Writing poetry is a creative and imaginative process, but getting it published is a very practical one. *How to Publish your Poetry* is a clear and detailed guide on how to get your poetry into print — for both the novice and the more established poet.

Beginning with the basics: why write? How good is it? Peter Finch systematically and thoroughly explores the whole range of essential topics including: preparation of manuscripts, dealing with rejection, available markets, copyright, self publishing, vanity presses, competitions, and readings and workshops. There are also useful sections on poetry bookshops, organizations of interest to poets, the poet's library and books on publishing.

A poet himself, Peter Finch runs the Welsh Arts Council's Oriel Bookshop in Cardiff and is an executive member of the Welsh Academy. He is a former publisher and editor, and is the author of a number of poetry collections.

Allison & Busby Writers' Guides
Published by W. H. Allen & Co Plc

THE MAGAZINE WRITER'S HANDBOOK
Gordon Wells

In this completely revised and updated edition of the companion volume to *The Craft of Writing Articles*, Gordon Wells provides an invaluable guide to more than seventy non-specialist magazines in the UK which accept unsolicited stories and articles. He examines the editorial policy and readership of each magazine with special reference to the opportunities it offers the aspiring freelance writer.

Clear and concise information is offered on:

- The subjects each magazine covers
- Regular features in each magazine
- Type and length of article required
- How long you can expect to wait for a decision
- Some idea of the likely payment

HOW TO WRITE STORIES FOR MAGAZINES
Donna Baker

Writing stories for magazines can be highly enjoyable, and with editors always eager for new writers it can be rewarding too. In this concise but comprehensive guide, Donna Baker takes the beginner every step of the way.

Starting with a definition of exactly what a magazine story is, she goes on to explain how to decide whether it is the best form for what you want to express. Then, in a series of clear succinct chapters, she shows how to develop characters, structure plots, use flashbacks and regional accents effectively, find the right market, keep accounts and, finally how to make the most of a word processor. This is a book that will be welcomed by the beginner and the experienced writer alike.

Donna Baker, who lives in the Lake District, is an established and experienced writer both of stories and romantic novels, which she writes under the pen-name Nicola West for Mills & Boon.